THE ✦ TIMES

THE QUEEN

AND

THE COMMONWEALTH

TIMES BOOKS

Published by Times Books

An imprint of HarperCollins Publishers
Westerhill Road, Bishopbriggs
Glasgow G64 2QT

HarperCollins Publishers
1st Floor, Watermarque Building,
Ringsend Road, Dublin 4, Ireland

First edition 2022

© Times Newspapers Limited 2022

A catalogue record for this book is available
from the British Library.

ISBN 978-0-00-854831-5

10 9 8 7 6 5 4 3 2 1

Printed in Bosnia and Herzegovina by GPS Group

Typesetting by Siliconchips

Thanks and acknowledgements go to Joanne Lovey and
Robin Ashton at News Syndication and, in particular,
at The Times, Ian Brunskill and, at HarperCollins,
Beth Ralston, Jethro Lennox, Harley Griffiths and
Kevin Robbins.

This book is produced from independently certified
FSC™ paper to ensure responsible forest management.

For more information visit: www.harpercollins.co.uk/green

THE TIMES

THE QUEEN

AND

THE COMMONWEALTH

CELEBRATING SEVEN DECADES OF STATE VISITS

Edited by

James Owen

CONTENTS

INTRODUCTION

"Must a name mean something?" Alice asks Humpty Dumpty after venturing through the looking glass. "When I use a word," he tells her, "it means just what I choose it to mean."

Alice's remarkable journeys were among the favourite reading of Queen Victoria – and the travels of her great-great-granddaughter, Queen Elizabeth II, around the Commonwealth have provoked reactions in her subjects which, over the 70 years of her reign, might be described as curious and curiouser.

They have ranged from uncontainable flag-waving excitement to something approaching shoulder-shrugging indifference. To evoke Humpty Dumpty once more, the reason for this might be the surprisingly varied, ever-changing, often uncertain understandings of what "the Commonwealth" actually means to each of its billions of members.

For the Queen, as so often, it has meant service. Her long, deep connection to the Commonwealth has been among the most vital and most fulfilling aspects of her life. As it has evolved from the remnants of the Empire, the Commonwealth's continued existence has enabled her to keep the promise that she made in the radio broadcast that marked her 21st birthday, that she would dedicate herself to the interests of all its peoples.

What has been particularly fascinating about her stewardship of this unique club, to which 56 countries now belong, has been to catch glimpses of her political talents, even opinions. At home, adhering to the role envisioned by Britain's constitution, she remains guardedly neutral.

At Commonwealth conferences, however, grumpy heads of state have been jollied up by her, and uppity ones subtly cajoled into line. Agreements have been reached and declarations made, if at times without universal conviction.

The Commonwealth has often been almost defined by its lack of unity, especially over highly divisive issues such as apartheid in South Africa, and frequently it has seemed as if it will rupture. Several countries have left, some of which have returned, with harmony restored. It is not by chance that the Queen has been there throughout, and increasingly central to the organisation's deliberations.

In between its meetings, her tours to every part of the globe where its members are to be found have preserved her more direct connection with its people. She has been the link between them and the sometimes-nebulous notion of a Commonwealth – the glue, it has been said, which binds everything together.

Yet despite the vast numbers of books published about the Queen's reign, relatively little has been written about this, one of its most successful achievements. This may be in part because of the passage of time, which has altered and eroded the ties that bound dominions and colonies so tightly to the "mother country".

It is an affection often amply reciprocated. But where once Australians and New Zealanders felt almost British at birth, when once a generation took ship from the Caribbean to help a Britain that already counted them as citizens, now the spaces between have grown bigger. The legacy of empire has become more disputed, and the purpose of an organisation which has persistently undersold itself not always clear.

What does it stand for? What benefits does it bring its peoples? How relevant is it to our world today? Does its existence imply constitutional ties with Britain, or boundaries? Not everyone appreciates, for instance, that when the Queen travels to many of the Commonwealth's most prominent members – Australia and Canada among them – she is not merely making one of her familiar diplomatic tours, she is there as their own Queen in what is still her realm.

As we celebrate her Platinum Jubilee, this volume commemorates the key role that the Queen has played in shaping and sustaining the Commonwealth, and the unfeigned affection it has always had for her.

Photographs evoke a now vanished if not always more enlightened age of global travel, while a series of short chapters survey the history of the Commonwealth's founding, the turning points in its history, and the dozens of visits that the Queen made over the decades to its constituent nations. Other chapters focus on its institutions, notably the Commonwealth Games, while extracts from contemporary news reports in *The Times* illuminate points of particular interest, offering informed perspective and occasional flashes of humour.

The same description might well apply to the way that the Queen has interacted with the Commonwealth all these years. Leafing through these pages, one cannot but be struck by the selfless dedication that characterises her public life, and by the deftness with which she adapted to the changing cavalcade that passed before her.

Above all, she has understood the subtle impulses which bring different peoples together, when it is so easy to find a reason to turn away. There are certainly challenges ahead for the Commonwealth when the time comes for her to pass the torch. Without her, however, its bright flame might have been put out long ago.

The new Queen, Prince Philip and their children wave from the balcony at Buckingham Palace after her Coronation ceremony in 1953.

A speech by the Queen on her 21st birthday

On her twenty-first birthday, April 21, 1947, Princess Elizabeth was with her parents and younger sister on a tour of South Africa. In a speech broadcast on the radio from Cape Town, the Princess dedicated her life to the service of the Commonwealth. The speech was drafted by Dermot Morrah, who had been sent out by The Times *to report on the royal tour.*

On my twenty-first birthday I welcome the opportunity to speak to all the peoples of the British Commonwealth and Empire, wherever they live, whatever race they come from, and whatever language they speak.

Let me begin by saying 'thank you' to all the thousands of kind people who have sent me messages of good will. This is a happy day for me; but it is also one that brings serious thoughts, thoughts of life looming ahead with all its challenges and with all its opportunity.

At such a time it is a great help to know that there are multitudes of friends all round the world who are thinking of me and who wish me well. I am grateful and I am deeply moved.

As I speak to you today from Cape Town, I am six thousand miles from the country where I was born. But I am certainly not six thousand miles from home. Everywhere I have travelled in these lovely lands of South Africa and Rhodesia, my parents, my sister and I have been taken to the heart of their people and made to feel that we are just as much at home here as if we had lived among them all our lives.

That is the great privilege belonging to our place in the world-wide commonwealth – that there are homes ready to welcome us in every continent of the earth. Before I am much older I hope I shall come to know many of them.

Although there is none of my father's subjects from the oldest to the youngest whom I do not wish to greet, I am thinking especially today of all the young men and women who were born about the same time as myself and have grown up like me in terrible and glorious years of the Second World War.

Will you, the youth of the British family of nations, let me speak on my birthday as your representative? Now that we are coming to manhood and womanhood it is surely a great joy to us all to think that we shall be able to take some of the burden off the shoulders of our elders, who have fought and worked and suffered to protect our childhood.

We must not be daunted by the anxieties and hardships that the war has left behind for every nation of our commonwealth. We know that these things are the price we cheerfully undertook to pay for the high honour of standing alone, seven years ago, in defence of the liberty of the world. Let us say with Rupert Brooke: "Now God be thanked who has matched us with this hour".

I am sure that you will see our difficulties, in the light that I see them, as the great opportunity for you and me. Most of you have read in the history books the proud saying of William Pitt that England had saved herself by her exertions and would save Europe by her example. But in our time we may say that the British Empire has saved the world first, and has now to save itself after the battle is won.

I think that is an even finer thing than was done in the days of Pitt; and it is for us, who have grown up in these years of danger and glory, to see that it is accomplished in the long years of peace that we all hope stretch ahead.

If we all go forward together with an unwavering faith, a high courage, and a quiet heart, we shall be able to make of this ancient commonwealth, which we all love so dearly, an even grander thing – more free, more prosperous, more happy and a more powerful influence for good in the world – than it has been in the greatest days of our forefathers.

To accomplish that we must give nothing less than the whole of ourselves. There is a motto which has been borne by many of my ancestors – a noble motto, "I serve". Those words were an inspiration to many bygone heirs to the throne when they made their knightly dedication as they came to manhood. I cannot do quite as they did.

But through the inventions of science I can do what was not possible for any of them. I can make my solemn act of dedication with a whole Empire listening. I should like to make that dedication now. It is very simple.

I declare before you all that my whole life whether it be long or short shall be devoted to your service and the service of our great imperial family to which we all belong.

But I shall not have strength to carry out this resolution alone unless you join in it with me, as I now invite you to do: I know that your support will be unfailingly given. God help me to make good my vow, and God bless all of you who are willing to share in it.

PRINCESS ELIZABETH

April 21, 1947

HISTORY OF
THE COMMONWEALTH

The Commonwealth is the offspring of the British Empire, with all the consequences implied by that filial relationship. If at times, as with the Empire, its parent has treated it with a certain indifference, so too the Commonwealth has had to work through growing pains and episodes of truculent rebellion towards maturity.

Yet while the nature of the ties has changed, the Commonwealth has endured, and the bond that its 56 members share with one another and with Britain is unique. Moreover, as has often been noted, its nurturing to adulthood has in many ways been the most personal achievement of the Queen. It epitomises her determination to dedicate her life to the service of those countries she was once born to rule.

At its peak, little over a century ago, the British Empire covered a quarter of the Earth's area, embracing almost 60 countries and 400 million people, a quarter of the world's population. The events of the C20th, notably the two world wars, would largely sweep away Britain's global power and influence, but even at its height the nature of the relationship between the nations that made up the Empire was very diverse.

By the late-C19th, the major colonies which had been chiefly settled from Britain – among them Canada, Australia and New Zealand – were already self-governing in most matters. Meanwhile, India, which because of its sheer size, much larger even than today, was treated as an empire in its own right and also occupied a privileged position.

Ranked beneath these in importance and in degree of independence were those countries which gave Britain its widespread reach, stretching from Kingston via Zanzibar to Hong Kong. Administered by British civil servants, the last additions to their number included those territories gained from the Ottomans after 1918, among them Palestine and Iraq.

The framework that was to come to determine the future nature of Britain's Empire was fixed in 1926 at an Imperial Conference in London chaired by the former Prime Minister, Arthur Balfour. Several of the self-governing countries had been agitating for more control of their own affairs, notably South Africa, Canada and the Irish Free State, then on its journey towards becoming a republic. Mindful of the revolution which had toppled the monarchy in Russia, and of the growing tensions in India, Britain began to make concessions to changed realities.

The conference declared that these large "dominions" were "autonomous Communities within the British Empire, equal in status, in no way subordinate one to another in any aspect of their domestic or external affairs, though united by a common allegiance to the Crown, and freely associated as members of the British Commonwealth of Nations." This formula, which gave the dominions power over their finances and foreign relations, was put into law in 1931 as the Statute of Westminster.

Dominion premiers and delegates assemble at 10 Downing Street for the Imperial Conference in 1926.

~ Status of the Dominions ~

Inter-Imperial Relations

TEXT OF CONFERENCE REPORT

The Report of the Committee on Inter-Imperial Relations, which was adopted by the Imperial Conference on November 19, was issued on Saturday. The members of the Committee on Inter-Imperial Relations, in addition to Lord Balfour, included the Prime Ministers of Canada, the Commonwealth of Australia, New Zealand, the Union of South Africa and Newfoundland, the Vice President of the Executive Council of the Irish Free State, the Secretary of State for India as head of the Indian Delegation, the Secretary of State for Foreign Affairs, and the Secretary of State for Dominion Affairs. Other Ministers and Members of the Imperial Conference attended particular meetings. The text of the Report is as follows:–

I. INTRODUCTION

We were appointed at the meeting of the Imperial Conference on the 5th October, 1926, to investigate all the questions on the Agenda affecting Inter-Imperial Relations. Our discussions on these questions have been long and intricate. We found, on examination, that they involved consideration of fundamental principles affecting the relations of the various parts of the British Empire *inter se*, as well as the relations of each part to foreign countries. For such examination the time at our disposal has been all too short. Yet we hope that we may have laid a foundation on which subsequent Conferences may build.

II. STATUS OF GREAT BRITAIN AND THE DOMINIONS

The Committee are of opinion that nothing would be gained by attempting to lay down a Constitution for the British Empire. Its widely scattered parts have very different characteristics, very different histories, and are at very different stages of evolution; while, considered as a whole, it defies classification and bears no real resemblance to any other political organization which now exists or has ever yet been tried.

There is, however, one most important element in it which, from a strictly constitutional point of view, has now, as regards all vital matters, reached its full development – we refer to the group of self-governing communities composed of Great Britain and the Dominions. Their position and mutual relation may be readily defined. *They are autonomous Communities within the British Empire, equal in status, in no way subordinate one to another in any aspect of their domestic or external affairs, though united by a common allegiance to the Crown, and freely associated as members of the British Commonwealth of Nations.*

A foreigner endeavouring to understand the true character of the British Empire by the aid of this formula alone would be tempted to think that it was devised rather to make mutual interference impossible than to make mutual cooperation easy.

Such a criticism, however, completely ignores the historic situation. The rapid evolution of the Oversea Dominions during the last fifty years has involved many complicated adjustments of old political machinery to changing conditions. The tendency towards equality of status was both right and inevitable. Geographical and other conditions made this impossible of attainment by the way of federation. The only alternative was by the way of autonomy; and along this road it has been steadily sought. Every self-governing member of the Empire is now the master of its destiny. In fact, if not always in form, it is subject to no compulsion whatever.

But no account, however accurate, of the negative relations in which Great Britain and the Dominions stand to each other can do more than express a portion of the truth. The British Empire is not founded upon negations. It depends essentially, if not formally, on positive ideals. Free institutions are its life-blood. Free co-operation is its instrument. Peace, security, and progress are among its objects. Aspects of all these great themes have been discussed at the present Conference; excellent results have been thereby obtained. And though every Dominion is now, and must always remain, the sole judge of the nature and extent of its co-operation, no common cause will, in our opinion, be thereby imperilled.

Equality of status, so far as Britain and the Dominions are concerned, is thus the root principle governing our Inter-Imperial Relations. But the principles of equality and similarity, appropriate to status, do not universally extend to function. Here we require something more than immutable dogmas. For example, to deal with questions of diplomacy and questions of defence, we require also flexible machinery – machinery which can, from time to time, be adapted to the changing circumstances of the world. This subject also has occupied our attention. The rest of this report will show how we have endeavoured not only to state political theory but to apply it to our common needs.

The Times, November 22, 1926

The wording avoided any mention of independence. Yet just over 15 years later, the British government would have to come to terms with India's inexorable desire to achieve it. Whitehall's chief concern, in the context of the threats posed by the Cold War, then became to keep India favourably inclined to Britain.

The leader of India's nationalist movement, Jawaharlal Nehru, was determined that the new nation would be a republic. There could be no question of it continuing to retain Britain's sovereign as its head of state, nor of it still pledging allegiance to the Crown. This seemed to be incompatible, as had proved the case with Ireland, with India remaining in the Commonwealth.

The solution was perhaps surprisingly straightforward. If India could not change what it wanted to be, then the Commonwealth would. At a conference of its prime ministers in London in 1949, it was agreed – following Nehru's own suggestion – that while India could no longer recognise George VI as its ruler, it had no difficulty in accepting him as head of a wider group of freely associating nations, as a "symbol of their unity".

This form of words would provide the template for the Commonwealth's future, a parasol flexible enough to offer shade to a broad variety of countries, republics and realms alike. It also encompassed different colours and cultures, as what had largely been a White club grew to include the three new nations of India, Pakistan and Ceylon.

Although the conference's declaration had been designed to keep India in the Commonwealth, it had in fact triggered the process of transforming the function of the organisation, from a group of subordinates to one of equals, as well as the role to be played by its head.

Prime Ministers gather for the London Conference in 1949 to discuss India's role in the Commonwealth.

(Left to right, standing) Stafford Cripps, Lester Pearson (Canada), Liaquat Ali Khan (Pakistan), Peter Fraser (New Zealand), D. F. Malan (South Africa), Don Senayake (Ceylon) and Philip Noel-Baker. (Left to right, seated) Mrs. Attlee, Pandit Nehru (India), Lady Cripps, Mrs. Malan, British Prime Minister Clement Attlee (and his dog Ting), Begum Ali Khan and Ben Chifley (Australia).

India to remain in the Commonwealth

The King as a symbol of free association of nations

An agreement enabling a republican India to continue full membership of the Commonwealth was concluded yesterday at the Prime Ministers' meeting in London.

While intending to be a republic India accepts the King as the symbol of the free association of the independent member nations, and as such the Head of the Commonwealth.

The basis of the membership of the other Commonwealth countries is unchanged.

DECLARATION BY GOVERNMENTS

UNITY MAINTAINED

The following declaration by the representatives of the Commonwealth countries who have been considering the impending constitutional changes in India was issued this morning from 10, Downing Street:–

During the past week the Prime Ministers of the United Kingdom, Australia, New Zealand, South Africa, India, Pakistan and Ceylon, and the Canadian Secretary of State for External Affairs have met in London to exchange views upon the important constitutional issues arising from India's decision to adopt a republican form of constitution and her desire to continue her membership of the Commonwealth.

The discussions have been concerned with the effects of such a development upon the existing structure of the Commonwealth and the constitutional relations between its members. They have been conducted in an atmosphere of goodwill and mutual understanding, and have had as their historical background the traditional capacity of the Commonwealth to strengthen its unity of purpose, while adapting its organisation and procedures to changing circumstances.

COMMON ALLEGIANCE

After full discussion the representatives of the Governments of all the Commonwealth countries have agreed that the conclusions reached should be placed on record in the following declaration:

"The Governments of the United Kingdom, Canada, Australia, New Zealand, South Africa, India, Pakistan and Ceylon, whose countries are united as Members of the British Commonwealth of Nations and owe a common allegiance to the Crown, which is also the symbol of their free association, have considered the impending constitutional changes in India.

"The Government of India have informed the other Governments of the Commonwealth of the intention of the Indian people that under the new constitution which is about to be adopted India shall become a sovereign independent republic. The Government of India have however declared and affirmed India's desire to continue her full membership of the Commonwealth of Nations and her acceptance of The King as the symbol of the free association of its independent member nations and as such the Head of the Commonwealth.

"The Governments of the other countries of the Commonwealth, the basis of whose membership of the Commonwealth is not hereby changed, accept and recognise India's continuing membership in accordance with the terms of this declaration.

"Accordingly the United Kingdom, Canada, Australia, New Zealand, South Africa, India, Pakistan and Ceylon hereby declare that they remain united as free and equal members of the Commonwealth of Nations, freely co-operating in the pursuit of peace, liberty, and progress."

The Times, April 28, 1949

This change would become more important over time, as the pace of decolonisation in sub-Saharan Africa increased rapidly, in part because of pressure from the United States. Ghana, formerly the Gold Coast, achieved Independence in 1957. Within a decade, all of Britain's other colonies in Africa, except for Southern Rhodesia, had followed suit.

The same held true for Britain's possessions in Asia and the rest of the world. Not all would join the Commonwealth – Burma did not, nor any of the countries in the Near East which had been protectorates, while opposition to apartheid led South Africa to leave in 1961. Nevertheless, by the end of the 1970s, membership of the Commonwealth had mushroomed to more than 40 nations.

British governments had originally hoped that the Commonwealth could be fashioned into a new vehicle for furthering their aims abroad and for cultivating trading opportunities. As it proved, Britain eventually preferred to join the EEC as a means of boosting its economy, weakening that historic tie with countries such as Australia.

Meanwhile, the Commonwealth's members tended to resist Britain's attempts to give it a political lead, for instance over how to deal with apartheid in South Africa. Indeed, one of the most notable features of the Commonwealth is how few policies it has succeeded in devising and seeing through.

If Britain did have influence, arguably it was around united values. It has helped to persuade the Commonwealth's members to sign up to declarations, such as that at Harare in 1991, which committed the organisation to world peace, liberty, free trade and co-operation. These were expanded on by its Charter, adopted in London in 2012, which set out its 16 core values, among them freedom of expression and the rule of law.

Queen attends Commonwealth event after recovery from illness

The Queen appeared at her first public event since she was taken to hospital with a bout of gastroenteritis a week ago when she attended a reception for Commonwealth ambassadors in London last night.

At the reception, held at Marlborough House in Pall Mall, the Queen signed the new Commonwealth Charter, which defines the core values that Commonwealth leaders endorsed last December, backing human rights and the rule of law in all 54 member countries.

With many member countries having anti-homosexual laws, the charter stops short of an explicit backing for gay rights. Instead it says: "We are implacably opposed to all forms of discrimination, whether rooted in gender, race, colour, creed, political belief or other grounds."

Earlier in the day, the Queen had cancelled an appearance at the annual Commonwealth Day Observance at Westminster Abbey. The announcement that she would pull out of the service but attend the reception is thought to have been influenced by the fact that the evening event was shorter and in the warmth of Marlborough House as opposed to a draughty Abbey.

Before the ceremony to sign the charter began, the Queen told guests, who included high commissioners from across the globe: "The charter I will sign today, on behalf of you all, represents a significant milestone as the Commonwealth continues its journey of development and renewal.

"We have now, for the first time, a single document that captures the core values and aspirations of the Commonwealth and all its members."

The Times, March 12, 2013

The Queen signs the Commonwealth Charter at a reception at Marlborough House in 2013. The Commonwealth Mace can be seen surrounded by the flags of the member nations.

Yet if its evolution was at times haphazard, and its continued existence even sometimes surprising, it is clear that the members of the Commonwealth believe their association bestows advantages. One proof of this is that its numbers have continued to grow steadily. Not only have some of the countries which have left it returned, notably South Africa, but its rules have been changed so that others can be admitted despite having no prior constitutional link with Britain.

Recent joiners include Mozambique, which was a colony of Portugal, Rwanda, and in 2022 Togo and Gabon, from historically Francophone Africa. There are now more than 2.5 billion people in the Commonwealth, almost a third of the world's population and very largely living in Asia or Africa.

Decisions by the organisation are taken by its leaders, who meet every two years at the Commonwealth Heads of Government Meeting, or CHOGM. The Secretariat, based in Marlborough House, near Buckingham Palace, and headed by the Secretary-General, is the Commonwealth's administrative agency and co-ordinates its activities and relations between its members.

Its other important institutions include the Commonwealth Games, the Commonwealth Foundation, which works to promote the organisation's values, and forums which support youth and women.

The one constant has been its Head all these years – the Queen. Ever since she made the celebrated speech on her 21st birthday in South Africa in which she pledged herself to the service of "our great imperial family to which we all belong", she has unwaveringly fulfilled her promise.

Her presence has often been vital to restoring harmony or to encouraging members to do the right thing, and she has played a more overtly political role within it than able to do in Britain. She has been described as the glue which keeps the Commonwealth together. Yet she has also learnt to adapt and be flexible in order to remain relevant and respected. The Commonwealth's challenge in the future is to do the same.

Princess Elizabeth makes a broadcast from the gardens of Government House in Cape Town, South Africa, on her 21st birthday   pledging her service to the British Commonwealth and Empire.

Delegates, government ministers and heads of state meet in Singapore for the very first Commonwealth Heads of Government Meeting in 1971.

56 COUNTRIES, 92 LANGUAGES: THE COMMONWEALTH

by Giles Whittell

At most of the Queen's public events, her subjects turn out in her honour. At several, however, it is the Queen who does the honouring, and each time the object of her respect will be the same – the Commonwealth.

No other institution except the monarchy itself bears the stamp of the Queen's personality as clearly as this sprawling collection of mainly English-speaking former colonies. It is not universally admired but in a sense it is her life's work. Its expansion has been her proudest accomplishment on the world stage, and it is no coincidence that most of its 56 member states are represented at her various birthday celebrations.

The Queen's role as head of the Commonwealth gives the lie to the notion that she is powerless. As leader of a vast group of nations with shared aspirations, she wields impressive power whether she likes it or not.

The Queen used this power most memorably in 2013 when, for only the second time in her reign, she did not attend the biennial Commonwealth Heads of Government Meeting (CHOGM). The meeting took place in Colombo. The Sri Lankan capital was recovering from civil war and its government was under condemnation for the deaths of about 100,000 civilian Tamils.

Aides said the Queen's non-appearance was not political. What did not need saying was that she was not going to fly halfway round the world to tarnish the Commonwealth by shaking hands with an alleged mass murderer. The effect for President Rajapaksa of Sri Lanka was devastating. In her place the Queen sent her son, and Prince Charles, in his main speech, avoided all mention of the civil war. He ended with a plaintive appeal to the "family values" that the Commonwealth represented. It was an awkward moment. Charles spoke for himself and his mother, and the subset of Commonwealth countries that successfully espouse democracy.

Overlooked in the fuss was the extraordinary fact that the Commonwealth exists at all; that it has expanded to include not just former British imperial possessions, but parts of Francophone Africa and a former Portuguese colony; and that it is the only international body apart from the United Nations to straddle the rich-poor divide on a global scale. The Commonwealth is loose enough not to break apart when stresses build, but coherent enough to function. It represents two billion people – more than a quarter of the world's population. It promotes democratic ideals even if not all its members practise them.

The Queen has been committed to the notion of a global English-speaking body since she was a young woman. Her first tour of the Commonwealth as Queen started five months after her Coronation, covered 40,000 miles and lasted seven months. For her Silver Jubilee she went farther: 56,000 miles. At 76, she marked her Golden Jubilee with trips to Canada, Australia, New Zealand and Jamaica. With very few exceptions she has attended Commonwealth summits not as an observer but as an exceptionally diligent chairwoman. She has made a point of getting to know other leaders, the better to anticipate their moves and moods. She has given hundreds of gifts and accepted hundreds more, among them a totem pole and a canoe.

Her father, George VI, had not taken the idea of a durable successor to the Empire seriously. As Richard Bourne, the former head of the Commonwealth Human Rights Group, puts it, running the Commonwealth "just wasn't as much fun as being emperor of India". The King's daughter was more concerned with duty than fun and understood that the Commonwealth had to be on the right side of history.

She had grave misgivings about Anthony Eden's bellicose response to the Suez crisis in 1956 and, according to her assistant private secretary at the time, may have gone as far as to remonstrate with him over his decision to retake the canal by force. She smoothed the path to Zimbabwe's independence, persuading Zambia's president Kenneth Kaunda to remove a potentially inflammatory reference to Robert Mugabe and Joshua Nkomo as "freedom fighters" from his speech at the Lusaka CHOGM in 1979.

Inspecting the troops of the Queen's Own Nigeria Regiment, Royal West African Frontier Force, which had been renamed in her honour before her visit to Nigeria in February 1956.

The Queen is greeted by children dressed in carnival costumes in Port of Spain, Trinidad, in 2009.

Princess Margaret, who had a house on Mustique, in the Grenadines, welcomes the Queen to the Caribbean island during her Silver Jubilee tour, 1977.

At the Taj Mahal in Agra during a visit to India, 1961.

She lobbied behind the scenes for democracy and against military dictatorship in Nigeria, and where democracy took root, she did her best to help it flourish. In one case highlighted by historians she was able to prevail on Ghana's charismatic president Jerry Rawlings to stand down at the end of his term (in 2001) rather than follow the disastrous example of some of Africa's self-appointed presidents-for-life.

Most importantly and courageously, the Queen sided with justice and the Commonwealth against Britain's own Conservatives in the long struggle against South African apartheid. It seems unconscionable now that Edward Heath defended selling arms to South Africa on the grounds that they would not be used to enforce apartheid and that Britain had an inalienable right to set its own trade policies. The Queen thought it unconscionable in 1971.

She consented with reluctance to Heath's demand that she should not attend that year's CHOGM in Singapore. The government tried to persuade her not to go to the next meeting either, in Canada, but she went anyway.

The rift between Buckingham Palace and Margaret Thatcher over South African sanctions was deep and enduring. Thatcher's refusal to back the embargo led to a broad boycott of the 1986 Commonwealth Games in a personal humiliation for the Queen. She continued to attend summits even so, including an especially difficult one in Limassol in 1993 when Greek Cypriots branded her a killer for Britain's hanging of nine anti-British rebels nearly four decades earlier.

By the early 1990s the Commonwealth was limping. It had split over South Africa, played no role in ending the Cold War and was sidelined by the Queen's own government as an annoying irrelevance for having the temerity to lecture Britain on its moral shortcomings when its members harboured plenty of their own.

Yet it survived. More than that, it thrived. Over the next 20 years South Africa rejoined after a 33-year suspension, and non-Anglophone developing countries started to apply for membership. For Cameroon and Mozambique it was granted in 1995; for Rwanda in 2009; and in 2020 the Maldives became its 54th member. Gabon and Togo joined in 2022.

A 2011 report by the preposterously named Eminent Persons Group said the Commonwealth was drifting from its reformist mission and was hypocritical over human rights. Undaunted, the Queen urged it to dust itself down, respond to new challenges such as food insecurity and climate change, and "stay fit and fresh for tomorrow".

The same year, the Commonwealth had a long moment in the sun on the Queen's triumphant 11-day tour of Australia that took in Canberra, Brisbane and Melbourne. She opened that year's CHOGM in Perth, observing that such meetings' importance "has always been in precise relationship to their relevance". It was a neat, disarming touch. The theme of the summit was "women as agents of change" and she urged all to continue to strive together to promote the theme in a lasting way.

The Queen had been met at the start of the tour by Australia's first woman prime minister. Julia Gillard, an avowed Republican, had refused to curtsy and bowed awkwardly on the red carpet instead. Aides said the Queen "couldn't give two hoots". She swept up all before her on her 16th visit to a country that has always reciprocated her affection. Before departing, she and Prince Philip were guests at a barbecue on Perth's Esplanade, attended by about 200,000 people.

Four years later, aged 89, the Queen resumed her role of leading the Commonwealth from the front. After the Colombo hiatus she took Prince Philip with her to host the heads of government in Malta. The trip was partly down memory lane, to a villa she had lived in before ascending the throne. But it was also the fulfilment of a duty to the Commonwealth she said she still cherished after more than 60 years.

The Commonwealth remains a popular and useful global forum – popular for the 4,500 athletes who competed in the 2018 Commonwealth Games, held on the Gold Coast, Queensland; useful for advocates such as Malala Yousafzai, shot in the head while going to school in Pakistan. The guest of honour at the 2014 Commonwealth Day service in London, Malala embodies the Commonwealth's ideals as well as those of the Queen herself.

Kenneth Kaunda, who was born in what was Northern Rhodesia in 1924, and lived on until 2021, once remarked that the transition from Empire to Commonwealth was made possible by the Queen's personality. "Without that," he said, "many of us would have left."

The Queen with Kenneth Kaunda, 1979.

Touring a market in the British Virgin Islands, 1977.

THE QUEEN'S
FIRST TOUR

1950s

A NEW ELIZABETHAN AGE

Commonwealth visits in the 1950s

6 FEBRUARY 1952

The Queen is at the Treetops game reserve in Kenya when she learns that her father has died, and that she has succeeded to the throne.

24–25 NOVEMBER 1953

The Queen and the Duke of Edinburgh embark on a post-Coronation tour of the Commonwealth which will last almost six months. Their first stop is Bermuda.

25–27 NOVEMBER 1953

They visit Jamaica.

17–19 DECEMBER 1953

After cruising across the Pacific, they arrive in Fiji.

19–20 DECEMBER 1953

They travel on to Tonga, where their host is Queen Sālote Tupou III.

23 DECEMBER 1953–30 JANUARY 1954

The Queen becomes the first reigning sovereign to visit New Zealand.

3 FEBRUARY 1954–1 APRIL 1954

The Queen and the Duke spend almost two months in Australia, where she is seen by 75% of the population.

5 APRIL 1954

They begin their homewards journey via the Straits Settlements, Cocos Islands.

10–21 APRIL 1954

The Queen visits Ceylon (now Sri Lanka), which was part of India before it gained independence.

27 APRIL 1954

The royal party stops at Aden, at the entrance to the Red Sea.

28–30 APRIL 1954

They make their only stop of the tour in Africa, crossing over to Uganda.

3–7 MAY 1954

Four days are spent in Malta, where the Queen and the Duke lived when they were first married.

10 MAY 1954

By now reunited with their children, and sailing on the Royal Yacht Britannia for the first time, the Royal Family dock at Gibraltar. Five days later they arrive in London.

28 JANUARY–16 FEBRUARY 1956

The Queen visits Nigeria for three weeks.

12–16 OCTOBER 1957

She becomes the first monarch of Canada to open its Parliament.

18 JUNE–1 AUGUST 1959

During an extensive six-week long tour of Canada, the Queen opens the St Lawrence Seaway, which connects the Great Lakes with the Atlantic Ocean. She also becomes the first sovereign to visit certain regions of Canada.

On November 19, 1953, Britain's Prime Minister, Winston Churchill, addressed the House of Commons. His subject was the forthcoming tour by the Queen, the first of her reign. Her 44,000-mile journey would take her to several of the leading nations in the Commonwealth, among them Australia and New Zealand, and right around the world. Remarkable as it now seems, she would be away from her home and from Britain for almost half a year.

"This will be the first time in history that a British Sovereign has circumnavigated the globe," Churchill told MPs. "Her Majesty, and the Duke, will set foot in many lands owing allegiance to the Crown and will no doubt arouse the keenest signs of loyal devotion...it may well be that the journey the Queen is about to take will be no less auspicious and the treasure she brings back no less bright than when Drake first sailed an English ship around the world."

The evocation of a second Elizabethan Age was deliberate. The tour was planned in some respects as an extension of the Coronation (which had been held in London in June), capitalising on the hopes and goodwill generated by the youth and glamour of the new monarch.

While India and Pakistan had already achieved independence, Britain still had a substantial empire and, less than 10 years after the Second World War, ties with former dominions such as Australia remained very strong. Some in Whitehall believed that through leadership of the Commonwealth, Britain could still be a first-rank global power. No-one had yet heard of Colonel Nasser, nor of his plans for the Suez Canal.

Transatlantic passenger flights had only started a few years earlier and the royal couple's journey began aboard a striking symbol of modernity, a BOAC Stratocruiser, Canopus. (The young Prince Charles and Princess Anne, meanwhile, were left at home). After a flight of more than 15 hours, including a re-fuelling stop in Canada, the aircraft landed on November 24 in Bermuda, then continued on the following day to Jamaica.

Although its newly elected chief minister, Alexander Bustamante, would later back the growing movement for independence, the island was still a crown colony and interest in the royal visit was all-consuming. In what would become a notable feature of the tour, vast crowds turned out to see the Queen, with 250,000 people – a sixth of the population – lining the road from the airport at Montego Bay all the way to Kingston. This was despite a heavy downpour. "It takes a queen to keep Jamaicans in the rain," observed one member of the royal party.

Accompanied by the Governor, Sir Hugh Foot (brother of the future Labour leader, Michael Foot), the Queen visited sites in the capital over the next three days. More crowds lined the streets and packed balconies. At one point, a gallant teacher, Daniel Warren-Kidd, broke through the barrier to lay his jacket at the Queen's feet, imploring her to walk on it over a muddy patch. The press inevitably dubbed him "Jamaica's Walter Raleigh".

At Sabina Park, the home of cricket in Jamaica, the Queen and Duke of Edinburgh greeted well-wishers from an open-top Land Rover. (Almost 70 years later, the use of a similar vehicle by her grandson, the Duke of Cambridge, when he and the Duchess visited the island, attracted controversy, with some commentators deeming it a throwback to the colonial past).

The Queen and Prince Philip smile at waving schoolchildren at Sabina Park, Jamaica, in 1953.

The new Queen is met at Heathrow in 1952 by (right to left) Winston Churchill, Clement Attlee,
Anthony Eden and Lord Woolton.

A royal wave en route to board the Stratocruiser Canopus to Bermuda in 1953.

The SS Gothic as it takes the Queen on the royal tour of the Commonwealth in 1953.

Jamaica greets the Queen

Big welcome at Montego Bay

The Queen and the Duke of Edinburgh came to-day to Jamaica and the Caribbean, a savage contrast in colour and heat after the demure, almost coquettish, beauties of Bermuda. Now the setting is tropical, and somehow more authentic; the November sun burns hotter and the sea is more vivid; there is a gay smile in the masses of flaming bougainvillaea, and an inscrutable, even grim air about the wooded ridges of the Blue Mountains which traverse the whole length of the island.

For a while the Queen will be on the old Spanish Main, which embraces so much of history and romance and bold adventure that began in another Elizabethan era. During her three days in Jamaica she will see not only the relics of those times but also something of their consequences and evolution.

It is eloquent of the forward march that the first voice of the West Indies to be raised in loyal greeting to-day should have spoken of federation and dominion status.

AIRLINER CREW THANKED

The Stratocruiser Canopus was above the green waters of Montego Bay comfortably before the appointed time, and there was not a cloud in the sky as it circled over the hills for its run in from the sea. The royal standard was broken in the breeze as the airliner taxied to the reception area, and on the stroke of the hour the Queen appeared at the door, looking cool and lovely in pale blue. A great cheer arose as she and the Duke came down the gangway to be greeted by the Governor of Jamaica, Sir Hugh Foot.

The Queen's first action, after inspecting a guard of

honour mounted by the Jamaica Constabulary, was to take her leave of the Canopus which, in fair winds, has brought her with such safety and precision to the Caribbean. She and the Duke of Edinburgh shook hands with Captain A. C. Loraine and the other members of the crew, for each of whom they had a warm word of thanks, and with Mr. Graham Bell, a senior official of B.O.A.C., who accompanied the royal party.

The flight of nearly 1,000 miles from Bermuda was made without a bump, and the Queen must have had some recompense for her early start in the thrilling colours of the sunrise over these sparkling waters.

The Times, November 26, 1953

The Queen at the door of the B.O.A.C. Stratocruiser in Jamaica, 1953.

Meeting officers of the cargo liner SS Gothic before her trip through the Panama Canal, 1953.

On the evening of November 27, the Queen set sail from Kingston Harbour aboard the liner Gothic. The Royal Yacht Britannia had yet to come into service, and for the next three weeks the Swan Hunter-built passenger-cum-cargo vessel was the couple's home as they cruised through the Panama Canal and across the Pacific towards Fiji.

Among the additional fittings added to the ship were safe storage places for the Queen's jewels, which included a pair of finely matched drop pearl earrings which had been a wedding present from the Sheikh of Bahrain.

Although she had travelled comparatively little before she came to the throne, in part because of the war, the Queen's shipborne voyage to South Africa in 1947 spared her a repeat of the customary ducking given to those crossing the Equator for the first time. Prince Philip, wearing a butcher's apron and with a red-painted nose, presided over the ceremony with gusto, welcoming first-timers to "Neptune's domains".

A delegation of chiefs came aboard as the Gothic neared Fiji, formally extending an invitation to the royal visitors in the form of a necklace of whale's teeth. After a tour by flying boat, the Queen moved on to Tonga, once known as the Friendly Islands. There she was met by her formidable fellow monarch, Queen Salote, who stood 6ft 3ins and had been the first head of state (before even the United States) to declare war on Japan following its attack at Pearl Harbor.

After a church service, at which a local choir sang Bach, the Queen of Tonga entertained her guests to lunch at her country estate, although *The Times*'s correspondent noted that "these conventional terms did not wholly describe the scene". More than 2,000 pigs were cooked for the feast, together with lobsters, chickens and yam, the whole washed down with coconut milk. In between meals, Prince Philip enjoyed a dip in the Polynesian waters, and he and the Queen were shown a turtle said to have been brought to the islands in 1777 by Captain Cook.

The Queen makes a film of Father Christmas

Meeting on the lawn at Auckland

Wherever the Queen and the Duke of Edinburgh have gone during these past four days they have received moving manifestations of loyalty and affection from the people of Auckland, who have often lined the route for hours in rain or sunshine, by day or night, to catch a glimpse of them. Tomorrow they are to begin their tour of the North Island with a visit to Waitangi, where the Maori chieftains will greet them on the spot where their forebears accepted Queen Victoria's sovereignty in 1840, thus bringing New Zealand into the British family of nations.

The strength of the links between the latter formed the main theme of the Queen's Christmas Day broadcast, delivered with serene authority from her sitting room in Government House – though perhaps its most memorable passage was her quiet disclaimer of the first Elizabeth who "ruled as a despot" and was blessed with neither husband nor children.

VARIED WEATHER

It was difficult to think of a "white Christmas" in Auckland, though short of that the weather has passed through some extraordinary variations from pouring rain and humid heat that brought down a batch of sailors at the naval review, to to-day's bright sunshine and cool breezes that took the Duke of Edinburgh sailing in one of Auckland's ocean-going yachts or "keelers" as the guest of Mr. J. Gifford, the commodore of the Royal New Zealand Yacht Squadron.

For the second time the Queen and the Duke of Edinburgh attended divine service this morning at the cathedral church of St. Mary, a small but fine example of its kind built of the wood of New Zealand's noblest tree, the kauri, which was so extensively ravaged in the old days that it is now preserved in permanent reservations.

The royal visitors had also attended Christmas morning service at St. Mary's; the Duke of Edinburgh read the second lesson, and they joined in the moment of silent prayer invoked by the Bishop of Auckland, the Rev. W. J. Simkin, for those injured and bereaved in the railway disaster.

EXCHANGE OF GIFTS

Christmas Day was spent quietly at Government House, with Sir Willoughby and Lady Norrie and their family, largely on the lines anticipated in this correspondence.

The Queen and her husband, with their hosts, attended Holy Communion in the bishop's private chapel, gifts were exchanged, and, after carols by a children's choir and a Salvation Army band, the royal party came out on to the lawn for a surprise appearance of Father Christmas, whose sleigh, drawn by six little ponies, was full of presents for Prince

Charles and Princess Anne – to whom their parents telephoned during the day – and for all the members of the household, offered by the women of Auckland, who also presented the Queen with a diamond-studded brooch of fern-leaf design, New Zealand's national emblem.

The Queen was clearly delighted, and she filmed Father Christmas's departure with her cine-camera, which, as the assembled photographers noted, she wields with an expert hand.

The Times, December 28, 1953

The Queen uses her cine camera at Government House, Auckland.

Just before Christmas 1953, when the Gothic tied up in wind and rain in Auckland, the Queen became the first reigning monarch of New Zealand to visit the country. Her arrival was to be overshadowed, however, by the deaths the next day of 151 people in a train crash at Tangiwai, the nation's worst such disaster.

Nevertheless, over the next five weeks, an estimated three-quarters of New Zealand's population turned out to get a glimpse of the Queen, as, in often rapidly changing weather, she visited 46 different towns and cities.

Perhaps the most telling moment of her stay came on Christmas Day, after Father Christmas had come to Government House on his sleigh – a sight the Queen thought "rather strange" to see in what was New Zealand's summer. That evening, she broadcast her Christmas message to the Commonwealth, outlining her own conception of its purpose and her role as its head.

"I want to show that the Crown is not an abstract symbol of our unity but a personal and living bond between you and me"

"I want to show that the Crown is not an abstract symbol of our unity but a personal and living bond between you and me", she said. On her tour, she had been impressed, she noted, by what the nations she had visited had built for themselves, but for her their greatest achievement was the Commonwealth. It was not like the empires of the past, but an equal partnership of nations and races to which "I shall give myself heart and soul every day of my life".

Other memorable episodes included the royal pair meeting Maoris at Rotorua, where they were presented with cloaks made of Kiwi feathers, and a four-year old girl boldly walked onto the dais where the Queen was seated. Those generations who knew only the older monarch might have been surprised by the one who let the child sit beside her for the rest of the ceremony.

The Queen makes her Christmas broadcast in 1953 to the people of the British Commonwealth from Government House, Auckland.

At the start of February, it was Australia's turn to welcome a reigning sovereign for the first time. As in New Zealand, about 75% of the population contrived to see the Queen over the next two months, as she visited 75 separate locations, travelling more than 10,000 miles around the country by air. In Melbourne, a million people thronged the road into the city, while in Sydney some 200,000 came just to see their queen go to a banquet. A peak of pride was reached when she opened Parliament in Canberra in her Coronation robes.

Officials had been worried about weakening ties with "the home country" and an increasing 'Americanization of Australia', but these fears were dispelled, at least for some years, by the evident strength of feeling on both sides. Aside from the devotion of many to the Queen, Prince Philip's easy confidence, as well as his interest in Australian technology, such as the nuclear test site at Woomera, earned him lasting favour.

The Queen and the Duke of Edinburgh touring Australia in 1954.

Inspecting a guard of honour at Prince's Wharf in Hobart, Australia.

The Queen in her Coronation gown, and Prince Philip in his admiral's summer uniform, after opening the Australian parliament in Canberra, 1954.

Sydney's day of celebration

The Queen royally welcomed

Its day of jubilation over, a weary Sydney went to bed to-night in the happy knowledge that the Queen and the Duke of Edinburgh were at last in the midst of its citizens, who will have ample opportunity of getting to know them during the 10 days before the royal party moves on to Canberra and the other stages of the two months' stay in Australia.

To-night the people in their thousands again flocked to the green, wooded banks of the harbour to watch a big display of fireworks. just as in the early morning they had assembled to watch the Gothic anchor in Athol Bight or, more to the point, to see and cheer the Queen as she came ashore from the royal barge at Farm Cove. It was here that the first Governor of New South Wales, Captain Phillips, landed rather more than a century and a half ago, armed with an assortment of seeds and plants with which, as prescribed by his warrant, to cultivate the land. To-night the floodlights picked out the British and Australian flags at the top of the soaring harbour bridge, and gave the illusion that they were suspended in space.

A WHOLE EXPERIENCE

A whole experience had passed since this noble steel structure had dominated the sunlit, sparkling scene in the basin as the royal barge emerged from the medley of small craft hugging the Gothic, with the air of a half-back breaking from a Rugby scrummage, and from the vicinity of an old fort, colloquially known as "Pinchgut," had entered the two-mile lane, formed by a double line of massed yachts, by which it reached the white pontoon reserved for the first official ceremonies of welcome.

The astonishing development of Sydney as the major industrial and commercial centre of the continent has in no way diminished the inordinate interest of its people in everything to do with ships, and no one surveying the scene in this, the world's finest, harbour would find it difficult to understand why.

The decorations, whether official or private, are on a scale and style beyond anything so far seen during the tour, and are said to have cost £2m. – and £10,000 was shot into the sky at the two-hour display of fireworks to-night. Many triumphal arches, in all manner of ingenious variations, have been erected, though one might miss the massed flowers of New Zealand, which, in the climate here, would wither all too fast. An outstanding example of skill is provided by an arch formed of four huge boomerangs; another depicts a great log, and at night the city is ablaze with illuminations such as have never been seen here before.

POLICE LINES BROKEN

The Queen paused to lay a wreath on the Cenotaph, where a crowd of 40,000 broke through the police lines and many people were in danger of being hurt in the rush as they were held back from the royal car. In George Street showers of streamers and torn paper fell on the procession from the tall buildings – a miniature version of the Broadway ticker tape reception, though in essential respects this is far less an " American city " than one had supposed. It seemed Australian enough as the great crowds moved along the main thoroughfares throughout the day, evidently bent on celebrating the great occasion even after the royal visitors had retired to Government House, and the trail of litter left in the wake of the crowds was immense.

The Times, February 3, 1954

The Royal Yacht Britannia moves through Tower Bridge, as the Queen, Prince Philip and their children return home from the Commonwealth tour in 1954.

The party journeyed home via Ceylon, which had recently gained independence, before stopping at Aden and going on to Uganda, to include Africa in the royal tour. Off the coast of Libya, they were reunited with their children after almost six months, the Royal Family then returning to Britain on Britannia's maiden voyage. There were stops on the way at Malta, where they were saluted by the Mediterranean Fleet commanded by Lord Mountbatten, the Duke's uncle, and where the royal couple had lived when newly married, and then at Gibraltar.

On May 15, 1954, the royal yacht sailed through Tower Bridge and, as dozens of small boats welcomed it back, anchored in the Thames. Cheering crowds clustered on the banks of the river, and more lined the streets for a triumphant procession through London, with the Queen's carriage drawn by six grey horses.

It had been a truly epic tour, as even banal statistics made plain. In travelling around the world, the Queen had attended 223 receptions, given 157 speeches and listened to another 276. She had shaken hands, it was calculated, 13,213 times, acknowledged 6,770 curtsies and accepted 468 gifts. *God Save The Queen* had been sung 508 times.

The objective of all this ceremony had been to reinforce the ties of distant peoples to the Crown by showing them their ruler in person, and in this it had undoubtedly succeeded. Times were changing, however, and nothing again would quite match the scale and grandeur of what was perhaps the last imperial progress. Nevertheless, it had been a most remarkable journey, even if it was only the first of many to come.

WINDS OF CHANGE

1960s

EVERY CONTINENT OF THE EARTH

Commonwealth visits in the 1960s

20 JANUARY 1961

On her way to India, the Queen made a stop in Cyprus.

21 JANUARY–1 FEBRUARY, 16–26 FEBRUARY, 1–2 MARCH 1961

The Queen and Prince Philip made the first visit by Britain's monarch to India since it gained independence in 1947. When in Chennai, the Queen cut a cake to mark Prince Andrew's first birthday.

1–16 FEBRUARY 1961

During their tour, they also went to Pakistan, formerly part of India.

9–20 NOVEMBER 1961

The Queen spent 10 days in Ghana, famously dancing with her host, President Kwame Nkrumah.

25 NOVEMBER–1 DECEMBER 1961

Her African journey also took in Sierra Leone.

3–5 DECEMBER 1961

The tour concluded in the Gambia.

30 JANUARY–1 FEBRUARY 1963

The Queen visited Canada on her way to the Pacific, refuelling in Edmonton and staying overnight in Vancouver.

2–3 FEBRUARY 1963

She went on to Fiji.

6–18 FEBRUARY 1963

The Queen returned to New Zealand for the first time since her post-Coronation tour.

18 FEBRUARY–27 MARCH 1963

A five-week tour of Australia took in visits to every state, including Northern Territory and Tasmania.

5–13 OCTOBER 1964

To commemorate the centennial of the visits of the Fathers of the Confederation, the Queen spent a week in Quebec before travelling to Ottawa, in Canada.

1 FEBRUARY 1966

After refuelling in Newfoundland, Canada, an extensive tour of the West Indies began in Barbados.

4 FEBRUARY–6 MARCH 1966

Over the next month, the Queen visited British Guiana, Trinidad and Tobago, Grenada, Saint Vincent and the Grenadines, Saint Lucia, Dominica, Montserrat, Antigua and Barbuda, Saint Christopher and Nevis, Anguilla, British Virgin Islands, Turks and Caicos Islands, The Bahamas and Jamaica.

29 JUNE–5 JULY 1967

The Queen made a state visit to Canada for the centennial of Confederation and for Expo '67 in Montreal.

14–17 NOVEMBER 1967

The first visit to Malta by a reigning sovereign.

In February 1960, Harold Macmillan, Britain's Prime Minister, who had been making a month-long tour of Commonwealth states, warned his South African hosts that a "wind of change" was blowing through the continent.

The decade that followed bore out his prophecy. More former colonies gained their independence, changing their relationship with Britain and with the Queen and altering the dynamic of the Commonwealth.

More broadly, the Sixties proved a watershed in attitudes and culture around the world as a younger generation, epitomised by President John F. Kennedy, asserted its discontent with the established order. Buckingham Palace had to

The Queen lunches with Prince Philip and their children Princess Anne and Prince Charles at Windsor Castle while being filmed for the BBC documentary 'Royal Family' in 1969.

contend with evidence of weakening loyalty to the Crown even in countries such as Australia and Canada.

Yet the Queen herself seemed to take these rapid developments in her stride. Deference was fading in any case, but the fact that in 1969 she permitted unprecedented insights into the home life of the Royal Family to be broadcast in a documentary suggested the process was mutual. Never one to look back, the Queen was less averse than many in the royal establishment to reconfiguring the relationship between her and her peoples.

At the start of the decade, her falling pregnant with Prince Andrew led her to postpone a tour of Ghana. Accordingly, it was not until January 1961 that she resumed her travels. She and Prince Philip then flew to Delhi for the first visit by a British sovereign to India and Pakistan since the two countries had become independent in 1947.

Their creation had led to that of a Commonwealth wider than the Anglosphere nations such as Australia and Canada. The Queen's tour would be a test of her belief that, as a living embodiment of its members' shared heritage, she could hold together the Commonwealth's increasingly diverse elements.

As republics, the India and Pakistan governments emphasised that she was being invited in her capacity as the Queen of the United Kingdom. There were worries on both sides that were her role as the head of the Commonwealth stressed then some might infer she had a residual authority over the former Raj, leading to protests. Indeed, her visit coincided with India's Republic Day, during the celebrations of which the royal couple were pointedly kept out of the way, and notably there was no playing of the British national anthem.

As it was, the reception that the Queen received showed that the anxieties had been misplaced. Some two million people came out onto the streets to see the pageant of her passing in Delhi, her carriage drawn by scarlet-coated grooms and shade afforded to the Queen by a regal red and gold parasol.

Reminiscent of her grandfather George V's imperial durbar in 1911 the sight may have been, but the visit also marked an opportunity to heal wounds and to acknowledge changed times. Hundreds of thousands saw her and the Duke lay a wreath at the memorial dedicated to Mahatma Gandhi. Still more listened to the mayor of Delhi refer to a "long history of conflict…ended in a unique manner honourable to your country and ours."

The most memorable moment of the tour, however, unabashedly embraced tradition. This was a private visit to Jaipur, where for her journey into the City Palace itself the Queen mounted an elephant. Swaying in a golden howdah, the Maharajah beside her, she processed to the great hall, where Rajasthan's gorgeously beturbaned nobles, their swords sheathed in scabbards of velvet, waited to pay their respects. Most of the women of the palace, however, were only allowed to watch the spectacle through peepholes, and the following day the Duke was taken to hunt a tiger, which he was expected to shoot.

The Queen riding on an elephant into the City Palace at Jaipur in 1961.

The Queen rides to palace on an elephant

Jaipur pageantry after welcome of Modern India

During the first two days of her visit the Queen has seen many Indias: in Delhi yesterday she was welcomed with the fond regard of the young republic; tonight she has gone back in time to the India her grandfather saw, and has ridden in triumph amid princely pageantry to the palace of the Maharajahs of Jaipur.

The Queen and the Duke of Edinburgh made the short flight from Delhi this morning, and their arrival in the capital of Rajasthan was almost a family affair by contrast with yesterday's multitudes. They were greeted by Gurmukh Nihal Singh, the Governor of Rajasthan, and the Ministers of the state government. The Queen, accompanied by the Governor, was driven into Jaipur in a vintage Rolls-Royce.

After lunch the royal party went to see an experiment and emblem of new India – a community development project in Bhankrota village. The Queen received the traditional welcome by nine young women bearing painted jars on their heads and a ritual offering of tiny lights on a copper tray.

PACKED STREETS

Meanwhile, the people of this city of miniature grandeur and infinite delicacy were gathering about the palace for the Queen's entry. Along the wide and ordered streets the people from the bare countryside were bustling in their holiday finery and taking up positions on the pink walls and balconies along the route.

The Queen, who wore a coat and hat of "Jaipur pink", drove to the palace through packed streets. Once within the great portals she mounted (from a platform) the noblest of half a dozen elephants, tented with silks and brocades and opulently painted, and, with the Maharajah beside her, rode into the heart of the palace.

From one of the courts there arose as she passed a giant twittering from thousands of women and children, but there were relatively few to see this progress.

After a banquet at the palace tonight the Queen and the Duke went by train to Sawai Madhopur where the Maharajah, their host, has a hunting lodge.

PLEASANT MEMORIES

When the Queen arrived in Delhi yesterday President Prasad, in his short speech of welcome, spoke of the association of the two countries and returned to it again at the banquet in the evening with the remark that, after the relations between the two countries had wholly changed in 1947, "the Indian people, as much as the British, elected to keep alive only the pleasant memories of their long association". His words and the restrained warmth of the greeting the Queen received from the people of Delhi struck the keynote of the visit: it is a level-headed and thoughtful affection that people here seem to be expressing for her, "as a charming young woman", as the Prime Minister put it the other night, but also as a symbol of the new Commonwealth.

The Queen's state drive to the President's palace took her through several of the many cities of Delhi. On the outskirts are the broken fragments of the cities of the past, forgotten tombs and disused temples, and here the villagers were gathered along the road, their bullock carts, prowed like boats, parked as grandstands, and camels, some with Union Jacks pinned like bibs beneath their resentful chins, serving the same purpose. The people had come in festival dress and the women and children looked like heaps of flowers as they sat by the road waiting for the Queen to pass.

Farther along are the modern houses of the well-to-do, where the gentry stood more self-consciously in tweeds and rich saris to wave their constrained welcome, and then the shops and office buildings and the young clerks in trousers and shirts.

Yesterday the Queen and the Duke drove to Rajghat, on the outskirts of Delhi, to lay a wreath at the memorial of Mahatma Gandhi – the first official engagement of her tour. Ten yards from the memorial they removed their shoes and put on velvet slippers to climb the steps to the memorial. They laid a wreath of 500 white roses, and then stood in silence for one minute in memory of Gandhi. The Queen planted a sapling in the grounds.

GOOD WILL GREETING

Among the 130 guests at last night's banquet was Tensing Norkay, who climbed Mount Everest with Sir Edmund Hillary.

In her reply to the President's address at the airport yesterday, the Queen said: "To all in India I bring a greeting of good will and affection from the British people. I hope that our visit will demonstrate to the world the respect and friendship which exists between Britain and India, and indeed between all the countries which are joined together in the free partnership of the Commonwealth."

The Times, January 22, 1961

India and Pakistan had shown the way in Asia, and it was Ghana which gave the lead to much of Africa. It had won its independence in 1957 and had declared itself a republic, but since then the British government had grown concerned about the country's future. In September 1961, during trips to China and Eastern Europe, its president, Kwame Nkrumah, had fiercely criticised the West's imperialist history, raising fears that he was preparing to move into the USSR's orbit. He had also repressed opposition at home and imprisoned hundreds of opponents.

The backlash against this, including the bombing of a statue of Nkrumah, had led him to fear for his safety when he moved around the country. In London, the situation prompted calls for the Queen's visit to Ghana in November 1961 to be cancelled, but she told Macmillan that she was determined to go.

She said that she took her responsibilities to the Commonwealth very seriously, and if one let those dwindle in the same way as her role as Britain's sovereign, then one might as well simply get a film star to do her job. Nkrumah had already felt snubbed when she had cancelled the earlier planned tour because of her pregnancy. What if she didn't go now, and the Soviet president, Nikita Khruschev, went a few weeks later and got a good reception?

So, rather bizarrely, the Commonwealth Secretary, Duncan Sandys, was sent out to Ghana to undertake a dress rehearsal of the visit. When both he and a delighted Nkrumah survived a drive through the capital, Accra, without mishap, Macmillan felt able to advise the Palace that the tour could go ahead.

Admiring the local fashion in India in 1961.

The Queen rides to a polo match with President Rajendra Prasad in New Delhi, India.

Vivid Ghana welcome for the Queen

Visit starts with emphasis on Commonwealth link

Accra woke up early today to put on its final glamour for the Queen's arrival. Schoolgirls dressed in crisp blue uniforms clustered for protection from the searing rays of the morning sun under trees along the route, and watched the final hasty touches being put to the displays by furiously working labourers.

By lunchtime the roads were jammed with vehicles and pedestrians streaming towards the airport, eight miles outside the city. Many of the lorries, bearing inscriptions such as "God be praised" and "People will talk about you", carried loads of cheerful people, who became more and more excited at the thought of seeing "this woman", as they call the Queen.

One of the gayest contingents among the crowds was a group of Nigerian women living in Ghana, who had passed the time while they waited singing and dancing. They were dressed in fresh-looking cloth, blue and white over wide-sleeved embroidered blouses, and their intricately wound starched headdresses curled high above them.

President Nkrumah's arrival at the airport was heralded by a fleet of about 60 motor cyclists, some wearing black uniforms, some wearing scarlet, and some white. As the Queen's aircraft landed and taxied round towards the landing steps delighted shrieks broke from the crowd and the group of Nigerian women broke into joyful song, while the chiefs' patterned and patchworked umbrellas were waved in the air.

When the Queen appeared at the top of the steps wearing a delicate *écru* lace dress and matching swathed hat, there were more cheers. She came down to meet Dr. Nkrumah, who was wearing a cream linen suit only one shade paler. The Duke of Edinburgh was in white naval uniform.

The national anthems of Britain and Ghana were played – only the second time the British National Anthem has been played here in public since Ghana became a republic – and the scarlet-coated guard of honour gave a royal salute, before being inspected by the Queen.

A scene of splendour and magnificence must have met the eyes of the Queen and the Duke when they stepped from the Boeing 707 airliner that had flown them from London fog to the brilliance of Accra. The regional heads and chiefs from all over the country were facing the runway attired in many-hued raiment of a breathtaking richness – kente cloths and robes barred, striped, and chequered, in brightest emerald green, orange, sunflower yellow, cobalt, and violet. On their heads were crowns and circlets of deep unpolished gold, or the occasional cap of fur.

The Times, November 9, 1961

The Queen and President Kwame Nkrumah of Ghana ride in an open-top limousine through cheering crowds in Accra.

Shaded by a suitably regal parasol in Ghana, 1961.

In her first speech in Ghana, the Queen laid stress on Ghana's membership of the Commonwealth and on its being a family of "all races and creeds...to which we are all proud to belong". More gestures of reconciliation followed, as furniture which had been at Windsor Castle since its seizure during the Ashanti wars in the late C19th was returned to what had once been the Gold Coast.

But the act which had the greatest impact came during the ball which marked the end of the tour. (Such was the clamour to see the Queen that a minister stole several hundred tickets to the ball and gave them to his friends: new tickets had to be issued.)

To the huge amusement of Prince Philip, Nkrumah asked the Queen to dance. Photographs of her doing so in her tiara made the front pages across the world, notably in parts of Africa which were still racially segregated.

Dancing with Ghanaian President Kwame Nkrumah at a farewell ball in Accra, 1961.

One newspaper in Ghana hailed her as "the Socialist Monarch". That may have been stretching a point. There was no doubt, however, that the Queen's visit helped to keep Ghana in the Commonwealth, not least since Macmillan was subsequently able to nudge Kennedy into financing the building of the Volta Dam to prevent the Russians from doing so.

Moreover, the Queen had shown that she would not allow the Commonwealth to become, as one Ghanaian commentator later put it, "a Whites-only club". She was, as Macmillan had noted, no-one's puppet.

For all their smiles in the face of whatever met them as they performed their duties, the royal pair had minds of their own. The Duke of Edinburgh would send his candid post-tour recommendations to ministers, for instance reporting after the Queen's month-long tour of the West Indies in 1966 that he thought many of the islands' governors too junior and inexperienced. He felt this put them at a disadvantage in dealing with the local politicians, some of whom seemed to admire African counterparts who had turned their nations into one-party states.

Yet it was not those countries which had newly won independence, such as Guyana and Barbados, nor those aspiring to emulate them, which began to give cooler receptions to royal visits during the decade. When the Queen returned to Australia and New Zealand in early 1963, local enthusiasm was notably more muted than during her tour a decade before, when people had gathered just to see her train pass during the night.

In part, this was due to the development of television coverage, which reduced the size of crowds. The main reason, however, was Britain's announcement that it would seek to join the European Economic Community. This promised to reduce substantially imports from the two nations to the "mother country" and was taken as a snub to their wartime loyalty.

In the longer term, both were also starting to forge new identities of their own, which looked less to the past and more to the future. The same was true of Canada, which with 22 visits was the nation that the Queen would journey to most often during her reign.

In 1964, protests by French-speaking separatists, violently broken up by the police, marred her arrival in Quebec City. The tour was also blighted by an accident in which the Queen might have been badly injured had she not refused to walk up the gangplank of Britannia after noticing it was moving. A few moments later, it came crashing down.

She returned to Canada three years later, when the country was hosting Expo '67 in Montreal and was also celebrating the centenary of its confederation. In her role as Canada's Queen, she attended ceremonies marking the nation's birthday, and even cut a 10-metre-tall cake on Parliament Hill, Ottawa. Always attentive to the symbolism of her clothes, that same evening she wore a gown designed by Norman Hartnell which featured on its royal-blue skirt a beaded band of silver maple leaves, the national emblem of Canada.

The Queen also visited the Expo, travelling to Montreal on Britannia. *The Times* lamented that to avoid potential demonstrations she was taken in and out of the exhibition site by a back entrance. Nevertheless, with Canada's prime minister, Lester B. Pearson, she enjoyed herself as they took a ride on the sightseeing monorail train, responding to criticism that she needed to let herself be seen more by young Canadians.

If the Commonwealth was a family, then during the Sixties it had successfully negotiated the challenges of childhood. There were, however, more turbulent times ahead.

Restraint in welcome to the Queen

Thousands of tourists, many of them American, poured into Ottawa today for the celebrations tomorrow marking Canada's hundredth birthday as a nation, celebrations at which the Queen and the Duke of Edinburgh will be present.

The Queen had a very good reception when she arrived at the Canadian armed forces air base at Uplands last night, and crowds estimated at about 60,000 lined the route into the city.

There was little cheering, for Ottawa people are not noted for open demonstrations of affection, but the welcome nevertheless was a sincere one.

It is very much a Canadian occasion. The flags everywhere are the red and white maple leaf and the gaily coloured centennial banners. There are few pictures of the Queen in shop windows as used to be seen in the past.

In spite of lowering skies, the Queen drove in a convertible car with the hood down to the wreath-laying ceremony at the national war memorial in Confederation Square today, and then went on to Parliament Hill, where she was greeted by large crowds.

The decision to travel in an open car was a wise one, because there have been criticisms here that in these royal visits the Queen is hardly seen at all in the back of a large saloon car, so that royalty is represented by something that flits by in a motor procession.

As the Queen reached Parliament Hill, members of the Rideau Club, a sedate institution with solid traditions, stood on the balcony facing the hill and clapped politely.

MEETING WITH PRESS

Inside the Centre Block the affairs of the nation were being conducted as usual. Questions were being asked in the Commons by Quebec members about whether shipping would be held up in the St. Lawrence on Sunday and Monday night when the Royal Yacht Britannia would be going downstream through the Seaway locks, taking the royal visitors to Expo '67 at Montreal and returning 24 hours later the same way.

Earlier today the Queen and the Duke met 200 members of the Ottawa press corps and visiting British and American journalists at Government House. It was a happy occasion and the Queen was applauded when she left.

The Times, June 30, 1967

Smiling at a Captain of the Guards at Canada's National War Memorial in Ottawa.

The Queen cuts a many-tiered cake commemorating the 100th anniversary of Canada's confederation, 1967.

The Queen takes in tall statues called 'Britain in the World' as she tours Expo '67 in Montreal.

GOING
WALKABOUT

1970s

GO FORWARD TOGETHER

Commonwealth visits in the 1970s

2–3 MARCH 1970

A tour to the Pacific and Australasia began with an overnight stop in Canada.

4–5 MARCH 1970

The two-month long journey got into its stride in Fiji.

7 MARCH 1970

The Queen, accompanied by Princess Anne and some of the time by Prince Charles, visited Tonga, where they met King Tāufaʻāhau Tupou IV.

12–30 MARCH 1970

A visit to New Zealand commemorated the bicentenary of Captain James Cook's voyages, and the Queen made her first informal "walkabout."

30 MARCH–3 MAY 1970

She then spent more than a month in Australia.

5–15 JULY 1970

The Queen and her eldest two children returned to Canada to mark the centenary of Manitoba and the North-West Territories.

3–12 MAY 1971

She and Princess Anne were in Canada again the following year to observe the centennial celebrations of British Columbia.

18–20 FEBRUARY 1972

Singapore was the first stop in a tour of South-East Asia and the Indian Ocean.

22–26, 28 FEBRUARY 1972

The Queen went on to Malaysia, accompanied at first by Princess Anne.

29 FEBRUARY 1972

Leap day was spent visiting Brunei.

2–8 MARCH 1972

The Queen visited Malaysia, then Singapore, then Malaysia again.

19–20 MARCH 1972

The Indian Ocean portion of the tour began in the Seychelles.

24–26 MARCH 1972

In Mauritius.

26 MARCH 1972

The Queen briefly visited Kenya, the president of which, Jomo Kenyatta, had been until a decade earlier a prisoner of the British authorities.

25 JUNE–5 JULY 1973

The Queen went to Canada and visited Ontario, Saskatchewan, Alberta and Prince Edward Island (the setting for the children's classic *Anne of Green Gables*).

31 JULY–4 AUGUST 1973

She attended the 2nd Commonwealth Heads of Government meeting in Ottawa.

15–17 OCTOBER 1973

After refuelling in Canada, the Queen departed for Fiji.

17–22 OCTOBER 1973

The Queen opened Sydney Opera House, in Australia.

28–29 JANUARY 1974

While en route to New Zealand, the Queen and Prince Philip visited the Cook Islands and opened Rarotonga International Airport.

30 JANUARY–8 FEBRUARY 1974

In New Zealand, they saw the Commonwealth Games.

11–27 FEBRUARY 1974

After the Games, the Queen visited Norfolk Island, New Hebrides, Solomon Islands and Papua New Guinea in February.

27–28 FEBRUARY 1974

The Queen had to cut short her tour and fly home from Australia, where she had opened Parliament, because of a General Election in Britain. Prince Philip carried on the tour into March.

16–18 FEBRUARY 1975

The Queen visited Bermuda.

18–21 FEBRUARY 1975

She then spent three days in Barbados, and another three in The Bahamas.

26–30 APRIL 1975

The Queen journeyed to Jamaica for the 3rd CHOGM.

4–7 MAY 1975

While on a visit to the Far East, the Queen travelled to Hong Kong.

13–25 JULY 1976

The Queen visited Nova Scotia and New Brunswick in Canada before opening the Summer Olympics in Montreal.

10–11 FEBRUARY 1977

She began her Silver Jubilee year with a visit to Western Samoa.

14–17 FEBRUARY 1977

The Queen spent a day in Tonga, before heading to Fiji.

22 FEBRUARY–7 MARCH 1977

In New Zealand.

7–23 MARCH 1977

In Australia, she took in the Centenary cricket Test match.

23–26 MARCH 1977

Papua New Guinea had asked the Queen to become its monarch in 1975.

26–30 MARCH 1977

In Australia again.

14–19 OCTOBER 1977

The Queen began the second leg of her Jubilee tour in Canada.

19–28 OCTOBER 1977

Towards the end of October, the Queen spent short stays in The Bahamas, British Virgin Islands and Antigua and Barbuda.

31 OCTOBER–2 NOVEMBER 1977

After travelling more than 56,00 miles around the world, the Queen flew home from Barbados on Concorde.

26 JULY–6 AUGUST 1978

The Queen visited Canada and also attended the Commonwealth Games.

19–22 JULY 1979

The following year, she made state visits to several African countries, starting in Tanzania.

22–25 JULY 1979

In Malawi.

25–27 JULY 1979

She went on to Botswana.

27 JULY–4 AUGUST 1979

She then travelled on to Zambia for the 5th CHOGM.

As the Commonwealth grew in size, so its workings became more complex. During the 1970s, the Queen would find herself embroiled, to a greater extent, in its politics. These revealed more clearly the ambiguities of her dual position as head of the organisation as well as monarch of the United Kingdom.

Nevertheless, the Commonwealth gave her more opportunity to display her diplomatic skills, and even her political ones, than she was permitted in Britain, where she had to remain studiedly neutral. And the addition of new members led to a rise in the intensity of her travel. In 10 years, she made some 60 visits just to Commonwealth nations.

These culminated in her Silver Jubilee tour of 1977. During two separate journeys, lasting 10 weeks, she visited a dozen Commonwealth countries, ranging from Western Samoa to Barbados. In Australia, she took in the Centenary cricket Test with England, and at the end of her travels returned to Britain from the Caribbean on Concorde. She had journeyed 56,000 miles in all, more even than she had on her great voyage after the Coronation.

Inspecting a guard of honour as she arrives in Barbados during her Silver Jubilee tour, 1977.

Royal visit marred by downpour

Heavy rain overnight disrupted some of the arrangements for the Queen's silver jubilee visit to Barbados, which began today. Because of flooded roads, many people who had planned to travel to Bridgetown, the capital, to watch her arrival in the royal yacht were unable to do so. Some outdoor events were moved because of the mud.

The rain caused power cuts throughout the island. Tourists who had left outlying hotels last night to eat in the town centre, found themselves stranded. Water poured through the roof of one of the island's luxury hotels. Many schools closed.

In spite of transport difficulties, however, more than a thousand people turned out at the airport to watch the landing of the Concorde which will fly the Queen home on Wednesday. Mr Adams, the Prime Minister, brought his children to watch the supersonic jet. The Concorde was a few minutes late, because it took time to fly over the royal yacht, some 35 miles off Barbados.

British Airways technicians had been slightly worried by a small dip in the airport runway which, they thought, might complicate the landing. It could make the front of the airliner bounce on its undercarriage, setting up a chain reaction. Nothing untoward happened, however, as the Concorde made a noisy entrance to the applause of the spectators.

An inspection inside the aircraft revealed that the Queen will travel in less luxurious style than that to which she is accustomed. Modifications have been kept to a minimum to allow the airliner to return to commercial service quickly. A small cabin, the depth of two rows of seats, has been set aside in the middle of the aircraft for the Queen and the Duke of Edinburgh. A number of seats in the rear have been removed, reducing capacity from 100 passengers to 45. This was partly to offset the aircraft's tendency to be heavy towards the tail, and partly to save fuel.

The Times, October 31, 1977

The Queen and Prince Philip during the State Opening of Parliament in Bridgetown, Barbados, in 1977.

The Queen and Princess Anne board an airliner at Heathrow Airport, London, at the start of a royal tour of Australia and New Zealand, 1970.

Her first tour of the decade, to the South Pacific, New Zealand and Australia, beginning in early March 1970 and commemorating the bicentenary of Captain Cook's voyages, was marked by a new informality. William Heseltine, an Australian who was then the Queen's press secretary, took up the suggestion by a New Zealand civil servant that when there she should spend time interacting with well-wishers and not only with dignitaries.

The first walkabout, as it was quickly dubbed by the press, took place outside of Wellington's town hall. The Queen alighted from her car about 60 yards from the building and walked the rest of the way, pausing to speak to some of those in the crowd. They soon overcame their surprise and its obvious success meant this was quickly adopted as a new royal ritual.

When the Queen subsequently arrived at Sydney airport, she and Prince Philip at once went over to talk to the mass of people waiting to greet them. Heseltine's initiative was so radical that, he later recalled, the scrum of photographers trying to capture this moment of royal evolution made physical progress along the line extremely difficult.

There was little time, however, for self-congratulation. Both Prince Charles and Princess Anne accompanied their parents on the tour. When the swirling wind caught the 19-year-old princess's hat, she made her displeasure known in frank terms which shocked some older Australians who heard them – and left Heseltine fielding their complaints.

The royal party spent more than a month in Australia, fulfilling several hundred engagements, although another welcome initiative was the reduced time for which the Queen was expected to speak. There were also the first appearances on these occasions of what became her characteristic asides and glancing notes of humour.

Carnival greeting for Queen in Australia

The Queen's first day in Australia since 1963 became a triumph from the moment she stepped from her car inside the Royal Easter Show ground today and went walking through a narrow channel between masses of people, preceded by a great bow wave of photographers, reporters and policemen.

Behind her came the Duke of Edinburgh, the Prince of Wales and Princess Anne. "Come over please, Queen" shouted someone, taking the sort of liberty which the more self-disciplined New Zealanders had taken only with other members of the Royal Family. The Queen smiled.

Before the afternoon was over she was moving happily through quite heavy rain, carrying an umbrella and a posy. All around her was that Australian family holiday smell of fried hamburgers and chips. Sometimes the crowd was behind barriers but in some places there were no barriers and it made no difference.

The general air of carnival and pleasant chaos affected even the formidable policemen of New South Wales. who customarily carry revolvers. They called us "gentlemen" and asked what won the Sydney Cup and did not mind if we could not give the answer.

It was, in a way, a brave decision for the Queen and the royal tour organizers to take up in Australia this "walking through the people" exactly where it had left off in New Zealand, because Australia is a different kind of country, with bigger, more volatile, crowds.

More than a million continental Europeans, many from Mediterranean areas and from the communist world, have come to Australia since the war and some have grievances. Would even one or two of them appeal or protest to their Queen? In New Zealand, peopled since the war largely by British or stolid stock from Europe like the Dutch, the question was not so compelling.

Also, to be honest, not all Australians like the "poms" and the kind of redcoat officer dominance which England's establishment used to stand for when the first fleet of convicts came out in 1788, only 18 years after the discoveries of Captain Cook, whose bicentenary this visit celebrates. There remains even now a residue of lack of interest in and distrust for things English.

It was noticeable today that the Canberra Times, the only daily newspaper published in Australia's capital, did not mention the Queen's visit on the front page. Partly, of course, this was a reflection of the federal structure here, with Sydney the capital of a sovereign semi-foreign state, but I do not think an American presidential visit would have been overlooked like this.

So this royal tour of Australia will not be a picnic for its principals although the overwhelming mass of Australians, new and old, have an affection and respect for the Queen.

Anyway, Sydney, big, brash and obsessed with the current boom, was the place to dive in, very much at the deep end, and the Easter show of the Royal Agricultural Society was the obvious place to begin, because here suburban Australia meets the bush. At the present time the confrontation is usually unfriendly, with the man on the land at odds with his government, which seems to represent the city, and rising costs in a buoyant economy for everyone else. Only last week 10,000 farmers marched through Melbourne protesting against "1940 prices and 1970 costs".

This did not impinge upon the show today when the Queen and Royal Family entered the huge five-acre arena in an open caleche escorted by 30 mounted policemen with lances. Heavy rain had halved the usual attendance but the cheers were loud enough.

On the three-mile drive from Government House the crowds were sparse and typical of any city on a wet weekend. The Queen's arrival at Kingsford Smith airport this morning had been preceded by a "southerly buster" which had swept bleak rain into the city from Antarctica and she stood for some minutes in the open in intermittent light drizzle while a 21-gun salute boomed out.

Once the official welcome was over and the naval band had been inspected all four members of the Royal Family walked across and talked with the crowd.

The Times, March 30, 1970

The Queen visits the Town Hall in Sydney with Emmet McDermott, Lord Mayor of Sydney.

Making the most of Australia despite the weather.

Walking with Prince Edward to watch Princess Anne compete in the Equestrian event at the 1976 Summer Olympics in Montreal, Canada.

Not all changes were quite so pleasing to her. The election of Edward Heath's government later that year not only meant that she had to deal with a prime minister whose manner she found less congenial than that of his predecessor, Harold Wilson, but also one whose policies threatened to break up her beloved Commonwealth.

Heath was determined to take Britain into the Common Market. He was much more interested in the country's relations with its neighbours in Europe than with its former and more distant colonies.

"Old friends will not be lost; Britain will take her Commonwealth links into Europe with her"

More controversial, from the point of view of the Commonwealth's growing number of African states, was his government's stance on apartheid. Heath showed little inclination to tackle White-run Rhodesia's continuing exclusion from power of its Black citizens, who formed the majority of its population. Still more provocative was his decision to reverse the previous prohibition on arms sales to South Africa.

This led to Tanzania and Zambia threatening to leave the Commonwealth. Heath accordingly advised Queen Elizabeth that she should not attend the forthcoming first Commonwealth Heads of Government (CHOGM) meeting in Singapore. It was likely to be stormy.

Heath's concern was that any criticism of Britain's position might also be directed at its sovereign, causing her embarrassment. In her constitutional role as Queen, she could not ignore the prime minister's advice and so did not travel to Singapore, although had she done so she might have helped to cool tempers.

Prevented by protocol from making her own point of view explicit, she instead found ways to do so more obliquely. In her Christmas message for 1972, she addressed Britain's imminent entry into the Common Market and the question of whether this would reduce the importance to the country of the Commonwealth.

"The new links with Europe will not replace those with the Commonwealth," she assured those watching. "Old friends will not be lost; Britain will take her Commonwealth links into Europe with her."

The text had, however, to be redrafted several times to obtain Downing Street's approval. The next potential stumbling block was the CHOGM meeting of 1973, due to be staged in Canada. Buckingham Palace ensured that there was no repeat of Heath's interference by having Canada's own premier, Pierre Trudeau, advise her in her capacity as the country's Queen that she should attend.

Compelled to entertain during the decade such dictators as Idi Amin, the Ugandan leader, and Romania's Nicolae Ceausescu, the Queen may perhaps have found her travels around the Commonwealth a welcome change.

Those to South-East Asia or Australasia – in 1973 she went to Sydney to open the Opera House – could take her away from Britain for over a month. In 1974, however, Heath caused another crisis during just such an absence. Unexpectedly, he called a general election, resulting in a hung parliament. This forced the Queen to cut short her stay in Australia and to return to London, where Wilson was eventually returned to power.

This proof that her duties as Queen of the United Kingdom trumped those as Queen of Australia fuelled republican sentiment there. The following year, her relations with Australia were to be set back still further.

The cause was the shock decision of the Queen's representative in the country, the Governor-General, Sir John Kerr, to dismiss the Prime Minister, Gough Whitlam. His government had lost the ability to get its budget through the upper house, the Senate. Kerr's position had long been thought largely ceremonial, but he felt that the political deadlock needed to be broken, as it might damage the economy and deprive civil servants of their wages.

Many Australians, already aggravated that they now had fewer rights in Britain than did Germans and Italians, saw Kerr's decision as unforgivable interference in the democratic process. Their assumption was that Kerr (who was himself Australian) must have briefed the Queen beforehand and had at least her tacit assent. Only 40 years later did the release of archived documents reveal that Kerr had decided he had no need to tell the Queen before he acted.

In 1975, to the surprise of all, the Queen gained a new realm. Papua New Guinea, which had latterly been administered by Australia, asked her to become its monarch and duly joined the Commonwealth. The Royal Family had visited the country the previous year and a spear-wielding Prince Charles attended the colourful independence celebrations, which marked the start of a memorable cycle of ceremonies.

The following year, the Queen, fresh from witnessing the commemoration of America's bicentennial, opened the summer Olympic Games in Montreal. There was apprehension about the reception that she and the other members of her family would receive in the French-speaking city – Princess Anne was competing in the three-day event – but it proved to be largely benign.

Buckingham Palace had at first looked askance at Pierre Trudeau, a premier not often troubled by self-doubt and one thought to be sceptical about the worth of the Commonwealth. At a reception for its heads hosted by Harold Wilson at Lancaster House, London, Trudeau, who had a penchant for such displays, surrendered to the temptation to slide down the banister of the great staircase.

It was Trudeau's levelheadedness, however, which had smoothed over matters at the Singapore CHOGM in 1971. The next serious crisis for the organisation would require the intervention of the Queen herself.

It occurred in 1979, when Margaret Thatcher's government was resisting calls for sanctions against South Africa. It was also deliberating whether formally to recognise Rhodesia, where the White regime was fighting a civil war against the two Black guerrilla forces led by Joshua Nkomo, based in neighbouring Zambia, and Robert Mugabe.

Such a move by Britain might have split the Commonwealth, and tensions were high before the opening of the CHOGM, which by coincidence was being staged not just in Africa for the first time, but in the Zambian capital, Lusaka.

When the Queen arrived some days before the summit, to pay a visit to the country, she was alerted to the intention of its president, Kenneth Kaunda, to make remarks critical of Mrs Thatcher at that evening's state banquet. She seemed to have taken matters into her own hands, persuading him in the course of their journey by car from the airport to avoid saying anything provocative in his speech.

Although at the time she was not allowed to participate directly in the conference, the Queen continued throughout it to exert her influence, holding meetings with the delegates. The Nigerians were mollified and the Australians exhorted to find a solution to the difficulties.

"Mainly because of her own personal involvement, tempers cooled," recalled Kaunda. The respect that she commanded helped stabilise the situation, and with minds focused, Britain agreed to host negotiations about Rhodesia's future. These led the following year to the birth of Zimbabwe.

The Queen shakes hands with President Kenneth Kaunda upon her arrival in Zambia, 1979.

Mossmen and mudmen greet Queen

Colourful warriors dancing at the Goroka showgrounds in the New Guinea Highlands provided the most spectacular performance of the royal tour of Papua-New Guinea so far. In nineteen different groups they provided visible proof of the diversity of Papua-New Guinea's tribal cultures.

Among them were the Asaro mudmen, who moved in ultra slow motion waving leaves round their clay-covered bodies. The mudmen cover their heads with clay masks in which the faces range from happy to sad and grotesque.

The Royal Family had intended to walk among the dancers but this was cancelled after heavy rain yesterday. One warrior presented an arrow to the Queen and another gave an embarrassed Captain Mark Phillips three of his arrows. Captain Phillips tried to return two of the arrows but was left with them still in his hand.

The members of the Royal Family took numerous photographs. Princess Anne waved her gold camera and politely asked press photographers to step aside at one stage. At first they did not react and she had to ask them a second time.

It was a case of the world's most photographed family finding camera subjects of their own; thousands of them. During a half-hour drive among the 5,000 Highland dancers the Queen, who also had a gold camera, Princess Anne and Lord Mountbatten took photographs of the people who had come to perform in their honour.

The Royal Family's fascination appeared as great as that of their subjects. Princess Anne, recovered from a cold which had caused her to cancel all engagements in Goroka on Sunday, was particularly interested in the "mossmen"; warriors covered from head to foot in fuzzy, yellow-green. After taking her photographs, the Princess reassuringly told reporters that her camera took good pictures.

In Port Moresby about 50,000 people, almost the entire population of the city, lined the seven-mile route from the airport to Government House. Thousands of school children waved Papua-New Guinea flags and Union Jacks, some of them handpainted as the Queen drove to the city.

The Times, February 25, 1974

Asaro mudmen greet the Queen, Prince Philip, Princess Anne and Captain Mark Phillips in Papua New Guinea.

The Queen and Prince Philip on safari during their state visit to Zambia, 1979.

The Queen and Margaret Thatcher attend a ball to celebrate the 5th CHOGM in Lusaka, Zambia, in 1979.

Posing with Commonwealth heads of government at the 5th CHOGM in Zambia in 1979.

COMMONWEALTH GAMES

One of the most distinctive and familiar features of the Commonwealth are the Commonwealth Games. Like the Olympics, they are held every four years in a different city, most recently in Birmingham in England, but what often makes them unique is the spirit with which they are staged. Historically, they have tried to foster a more fraternal, less relentlessly competitive approach to sport, and they cherish their appellation as "the friendly games".

The idea of putting on a competition of sporting prowess to show the unity between the various countries of the then British Empire was mooted as early as the late C19th. An Australian-born clergyman, John Astley Cooper, wrote to *The Times* in 1891, calling for a "Pan-Britannic-Pan Anglican Contest and Festival." His aim, in part, was to identify talented students from the dominions, and this suggestion is said to have inspired the foundation of the Rhodes scholarships at Oxford University.

Nothing came of Cooper's idea for some time, but it did encourage Pierre de Coubertin, who worried that non-Empire athletes would be excluded from such a contest, to found the modern Olympic Games in 1894.

Then, in 1911, an "Inter Empire Sports Meeting" was held at the Crystal Palace in London under the auspices of the Festival of Empire that marked the Coronation of George V. Sportsmen – and they were then all men – from four nations took part in nine events. Although there was some criticism in the press of the limited nature of the tournament, Canada was judged to have finished top and its team was presented with a vast silver trophy. This was later melted down, and one of the cups made from it is now kept by the Commonwealth Games Federation which organises the competition.

The proposed Pan-Britannic or Pan-Anglican Contest and Festival

To the Editor of *The Times*

Sir, my plan to obtain an English federal sign outside of existing political and commercial organizations has been so much misrepresented, owing most probably to Mr. Froude's reference to the old Greek Pan-Athenaion in his published letter approving of my plan, that I have to ask your permission to state as exactly as I can in a small space in what way I propose to bring about a common periodical representative gathering of the English people, and to establish a national festival probably every four years.

I propose as a means of increasing the good will and the good understanding of the Empire, also with the hope of drawing closer the family bonds between the United States and the Empire of the Queen, a periodical gathering of representatives of the race in a festival and contest of industry, athletics, and culture.

In suggesting the next section of the contest, that of athletics, I have taken into consideration the fact that the future relationship of the various portions of the Empire rests chiefly in the hands of the young men of the Empire – of young England, young Australia, young South Africa, young Canada – and that an Imperial athletic contest would be very attractive to most Englishmen, whether settled in the United Kingdom or resident beyond the seas. I also believe that such a contest between carefully selected representatives of the English-speaking race would command more general attention and be more popular than any other contest which could be arranged. I am supported in this by the fact that the home Press and the colonial Press who have passed criticisms on my scheme, such as they surmised it to be, have been unanimous on this point. I would suggest that the contests should not be further extended than to running, rowing, and cricket. Respecting the rowing and running contests, I am assured that if the contest was arranged under national and Imperial auspices the premier clubs of the Empire and of America would not hesitate to bear the expenses of their champions; and, to quote a letter received last Saturday from Melbourne, "If preliminary contests were held in each part of the dominions, there might be a sifting of competitors which would improve the final efforts and limit the area of actual competition." I should say that two representatives from each part of the Empire, or perhaps three in case of illness, say from England, Scotland, Ireland, Wales, Canada, Australia, and South Africa, would be quite sufficient to represent in each event. Perhaps one or more divisions of the Empire would send none for certain events if really good men were not forthcoming. In the above remarks I have been thinking chiefly of the contests on the cinder-path. As regards rowing, Australia and Canada might send one eight each after preliminary competitions in each country, with reserve men, and two or three representative scullers each to contest with the mother country over the Putney and Mortlake course. In cricket a series of most interesting matches could be arranged and played on the London grounds, and I have no doubt that the colonial teams could so arrange a tour that both previous to and after the national and Imperial games they could pay their own expenses. If not, the sportsmen of the Empire would see that the representatives of Australia, Canada, and the Cape were no losers. I propose that all these contests of running, rowing, and cricket take place in the month of June in or near London.

The prizes for the victors in this Imperial athletic contest have been a subject of much anxious thought, and, after consultation with several leading and genuine sportsmen, I suggest that no money prizes be given at all, but that instead some symbolic trophy be given to the victor in each event of the athletic contests – some gift from the nation or the race to the man, which would be treasured. I need not point out that though that Imperial gift was of the simplest character in itself, still it would confer not only fame and honour, but there would be in it the elements of fortune and a successful career, if properly and judiciously utilized in the land which the winner represented. I think that the American athletes could well be invited to join in this English-speaking family gathering for sport, and no one would grudge them a well-earned victory.

Believe me, yours faithfully,

J. ASTLEY COOPER

The Times, October 30, 1891

The Queen presents the silver medal for the high jump to Ann Wilson of England, as gold medallist Debbie Brill of Canada looks on, during the 1970 Commonwealth Games in Edinburgh.

The Games were not put on a more regular footing, however, until 1930. That year, at the initiative of the manager of Canada's athletics team, Bobby Robinson, the British Empire Games was held in the city of Hamilton, Ontario. There were 400 competitors from nine countries, among them Newfoundland, Bermuda and Northern Ireland (the United Kingdom still splits into its different nations for the Games today). Women, however, only took part in the swimming and diving events.

Among the other four sports contested was lawn bowls, and the more relaxed nature of the Games was apparent from the start. When a New Zealand athlete was disqualified after two false starts in the 100 yards, the spectators loudly made their feelings felt until he was reinstated.

The Games were opened by Canada's Governor-General, who read out a message from the King. This royal connection has remained strong ever since. The Queen has attended most of the Games held during her reign, and when she was not able to open them, the Duke of Edinburgh would read her message. Their children have also frequently been seen at the Games.

Over the years, other rituals have developed at the Games. The most notable perhaps is the Queen's Baton Rally, which was instituted at Cardiff in 1958 and modelled on the journey of the Olympic torch. On the first occasion, the Queen passed a silver baton containing her message to a cohort of runners that included Roger Bannister and Christopher Chataway, who carried it from Buckingham Palace to the stadium in Wales.

The longest relay since came in 2018 as, over the course of more than a year, the baton travelled 150,000 miles around the world, through the different parts of the Commonwealth, until it reached Australia's Gold Coast.

The Games have had several changes of name, finally settling on the present one in 1974. There have also been other iterations of it. A winter version was staged at St Moritz, in Switzerland, three times in the late 1950s and 1960s. An event for paraplegic athletes was held between 1962 and 1974, and athletes with a disability have since 2002 competed as part of their national teams at the Games. A quadrennial Youth Games, for those aged between 14 and 18, was inaugurated in 2000.

Prince Philip receives the baton containing the Queen's message from Ken Jones
at the opening of the 1958 British Empire Games in Cardiff.

England football captain David Beckham and Kirsty Howard hand the baton to the Queen at the opening of the 2002 Commonwealth Games in Manchester.

The Empire Games

To-day's opening at Hamilton

The first Empire Games will begin at the Stadium here to-morrow afternoon at half-past 5, after the formal opening by the Governor-General, Lord Willingdon, the famous Eton and Cambridge cricketer. Over 400 Empire athletes will parade round the track, each wearing the uniform of his team. The athletic contests will then begin, and in the evening the first swimming events will be held in the municipal baths.

These are the first Empire Games that have ever been held, and they have been organized by Mr. M. Robinson, a Hamiltonian with a long experience of every branch of sport, who led the Canadians at the Olympic Games at Amsterdam. He then conceived this idea, on which he has worked since. He has had the hearty cooperation of Mr. E. W. Beatty, president of the Canadian Pacific Railway, who is a strong believer in amateur sport. The competitors represent every part of the Empire – England, Scotland, Ireland, Wales, Canada, Australia, New Zealand, South Africa, Newfoundland, Bermuda, British Guiana – and they will meet on the track, on the field, at rowing, swimming, boxing, wrestling, and bowls. It is hoped that the Games will help to promote ties of fellowship and good will in the Empire, bringing as they do so many prominent members of the younger generation together. It is also hoped that they will assist in the formation of an Empire sports federation to maintain the high standard and traditions of sportsmanship. Other contests held during the week include Canadian canoe championships and international canoe championships, this being the first time that such meetings have been held. There will also be contests between the United States and Canada at rowing, yachting, and skiff racing, the Canadian women's athletic championships, and the Ontario schoolboy championships.

At the close of the Games the Empire team will be selected to meet the United States at Soldiers' Field, Chicago, during the following week. Many famous athletes are already present for the Games, among them being Percy Williams, of Vancouver, the double Olympic champion, who made a new world's record for the 100 metres at Toronto last Saturday without being pressed. It is hoped that he may do better at the Games.

Unfortunately the British athletic team, who sailed in the Duchess of Atholl, were delayed by fog and so arrived here only last night, and have but one day to recover their land legs after their long sea voyage and train journey. All the athletes are housed together at the City's expense in the Prince of Wales School. Adjoining the Stadium, with the baths not far distant.

The rowing events are to be held in a bay on Lake Ontario at the end of which lies Hamilton. It is a wonderful naturally made position, with a sand-spit running across the bay, which accommodates 1,000 spectators. If the wind is off-shore the races will be held outside, but if it is blowing off the lake the races will be inside in sheltered waters. Hamilton suffered recently, like a great part of the United States, from a prolonged drought, and there is little green to be seen, the track being somewhat hard, but last night a heavy rainstorm improved the conditions.

Hamilton City has played a great part in Dominion sport, having produced great football teams, runners, and rowers. The City streets are bedecked with flags, and the hotels are crowded with visitors for the opening day. Among those who will attend will be the Prime Minister, who to-day addressed the opening meeting of the Canadian and British Bar, at which many distinguished British Judges and barristers were present.

The Times, August 16, 1930

Although thousands of athletes now participate in the Games, and despite the medal table tending to be dominated by nations such as Australia and England, one achievement of the Games has been to give experience and exposure to future stars from smaller or less wealthy countries.

Some 72 have been represented at the Games – among them individual territories and dependencies of what are now the 56 members – and these have included, for instance, the great middle-distance runners from Kenya who went on in the 1970s to become world famous.

There have been many memorable moments over the years. The second staging of the Games was in London, a switch from the original host, Johannesburg, after concern grew about the way that Asian and Black athletes might be treated there.

Memories of an earlier controversy were revived four years later when the opening ceremony of the Games was held at the Sydney Cricket Ground, where the bodyline cricket series had marred relations between Australia and England five years before. Fiji and Ceylon made their first appearances, but to the delight of the locals Australia saw off England to head the medal table.

The Second World War meant that the next Games did not take place until 1950. Almost 600 athletes travelled to Auckland, among them England's Jack Holden, who won the marathon at the age of 43 after being chased by a dog – a Great Dane in some accounts – and after running the last nine miles in bare feet when his shoes fell apart.

There was more drama in the marathon four years later in Vancouver. The world record holder, England's Jim Peters, entered the stadium with a lead of 17 minutes, and 10 minutes ahead of the schedule needed to set a new record.

He had only a single lap to run but was so exhausted that he collapsed eleven times as he vainly struggled to reach the tape. He never raced again. The Games are also remembered for one of the greatest ever mile races, as both Roger Bannister and Australia's John Landy ran times under the recently broken four-minute mark.

The likes of Australia's middle-distance runner Herb Elliot and swimmer Dawn Fraser emerged as stars at the 1958 Games in Cardiff, but they were overshadowed by what was to become another regular feature of the competition, protests about racial equality.

Prior to the opening ceremony, prominent sportsmen such as footballers Stanley Matthews and Jimmy Hill signed a letter to *The Times* criticising the decision by South Africa to select its athletes on the basis of their skin colour. More African countries than ever took part in the Games, and South Africa left the Commonwealth three years later.

Later, there were boycotts of the Games when countries who maintained sporting links with South Africa competed, and in 1977 the Gleneagles Agreement largely severed those which remained. As in the organisation as a whole, apartheid proved to be a fault line and a bar to unity.

At the 1962 Games in Perth, Dawn Fraser won two more golds, although Anita Lonsborough of England won three in the pool. Australia's Peter Snell succeeded Elliott as champion in the 880-yards, while Kip Kcino heralded the arrival of the Kenyans with victory over both one and three miles. The Games closed with the athletes, watched by Prince Philip, marching out of the stadium, arm-in-arm, as a 700-strong choir sang Waltzing Matilda.

England's Roger Bannister leads Australia's John Landy, breaking the tape to win the mile event at the 1954 British Empire Games in Vancouver.

The medallists in the 6-mile race: (left to right) Frank Sando, Peter Driver and Jim Peters on the rostrum at the 1954 British Empire Games in Vancouver.

Australian swimmer Dawn Fraser in training for the 1962 British Empire and Commonwealth Games in Perth.

Friendly Games
end with a "Boomer"

Back to beaches at Perth

"It's a boomer, isn't it?" asked our host, and last night's theoretically private party in Floreat Park certainly was a success, as swimmers, boxers, athletes and camp followers twisted and feasted until dawn. But today this is a city with a hangover so far as organized sport is concerned and the natives have gone back to the white beaches to tan their bodies under the sun.

Many of the competitors have already flown away, back to their respective corners of the earth, and now the stadium, the swimming pool and the village look deserted. There is nothing new in this, for so it was at the Melbourne Olympics in 1956, at Cardiff in 1958, and at Rome two years ago. But each time a great sporting festival quietly dies the transience of all such affairs comes to mind:–

Golden lads and girls all must.
As chimney sweepers, come to
dust.

Golden they have been at these Games, with the sun leaving some enervated and others stimulated, but always a suitable background to a splendid occasion. The weather changed, mercifully, for the marathon and those from the United Kingdom cannot reckon that the hot climate had too much to do with the final results. In most ways the form book was proved reliable and the weather made little mockery of natural ability.

Judging from the highest competitive standard, the Games were, perhaps, a little disappointing. The boxing, it is generally agreed, was marred by inept adjudicating. The swimming produced world records, but the Australian men's team, so predominant, lacked real opposition. The athletics provided healthy competition, but we saw no new peaks of human endeavour.

BARBECUE'S GLOW

But all such carping counts for little by comparison with the overwhelming impression of friendliness that has characterized these Games. Only, perhaps, in Vancouver in 1954 have visitors been greeted with the same warmth. Last night, as the house in Floreat Park which had given a party every other night for a fortnight jumped for joy, the young faces glowed in the light of a barbecue fire and 100 gallons of ale washed away the tensions of competition. The phrase "The Friendly Games" had become a truism rather than a cliché.

In the same way it is not just the dashes for the tape, the desperate lunges of the fencer, and the acrobatics of the diver that provide my clearest memory. It is, rather, the pleasant company at the swimming pool, the friendly wagering at the athletics and the intimate, sometimes blood-tinged atmosphere

of post-mortem examination and commiseration in the boxing dressing rooms that emphasizes what Perth 1962 was for those of us privileged to watch.

It was the same spontaneity which characterizes youth and sport which rescued the closing ceremony from the rather hollow, militaristic mood which threatened it. The squad of soldiers standing to attention in the centre of the main stadium was a miserable lapse in taste, but their unnecessary presence – which caused someone to suggest there was a secret rocket-launching pad under the tarpaulin covering the high jump pit – was soon underlined.

BOXER WITH BATON

The competitors marched round the track led by a rebel group, headed by the Australian runner A. G. Thomas wearing an English track suit. They carried official signs bearing such devices as "City of Perth Official Parking", and "Post Office", and the hammer thrower H. W. Payne was even holding an ice-cream tray. Three Australians staggered along bowed under an 8ft. board advertising tickets, and a Jamaican toured the track on a racing cycle with an Australian woman swimmer on the crossbar.

In spite of the efforts of non-commissioned officers, who should never have been sent on to the centre in the first place, the competitors weaved their own merry way, to the delight of the crowd. James, the Welsh heavyweight boxer, took over a baton and conducted the choir from the rostrum in company with Miss Shirley, the English high jumper. As thousands roared with laughter the military remained at rigid attention. Fortunately, no competitor thought of taking one of their rifles as a souvenir.

The Times, December 3, 1962

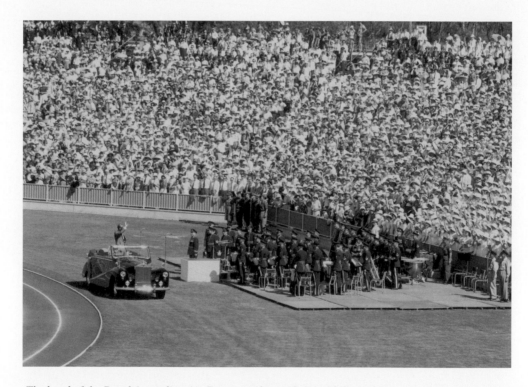

The band of the Royal Australian Air Force watches as Prince Philip is driven round the arena at the start of the 1962 British Empire and Commonwealth Games in Perth.

*Athletes from all corners of the Commonwealth enjoy the atmosphere
at the Melbourne 2006 Commonwealth Games.*

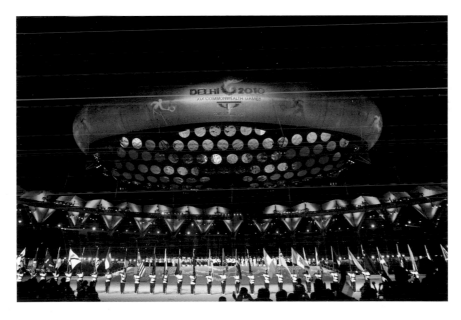

*Flagbearers from the Commonwealth nations stand during the Opening Ceremony
for the Delhi 2010 Commonwealth Games.*

After Jamaica had become the first country with a majority Black population to host the event – the first to be known as the British Commonwealth rather than Empire Games – it was the turn of Edinburgh. Metric distances replaced imperial ones and more countries than ever tasted gold, among them Hong Kong, Malaysia, Pakistan, Jamaica and a clutch of African nations. In the first 1500m race contested by female athletes, New Zealand would have claimed gold had not an exhausted Sylvia Potts collapsed a yard from the finishing line.

Held in Edmonton, Canada, and remembered for Graham Smith's six victories in the pool, the 1978 Commonwealth Games were the first to use that name. Nigeria boycotted them, however, to protest at New Zealand's continued sporting ties with South Africa. A total of 32 countries would boycott those of 1986, held again in Edinburgh.

The media tycoon Robert Maxwell volunteered to make up the considerable shortfall in funding for the Games but failed to deliver on his promise. Meanwhile, spectators were treated to notable achievements by Daley Thompson, Linford Christie, Steve Cram, Steve Redgrave, Lennox Lewis and Liz McColgan.

The Queen and Prince Philip at the opening of the 1978 Commonwealth Games in Edmonton, Canada.

The tide turned in the Nineties, as a record 55 countries took part in the Games in Auckland and South Africa returned to competition at the following staging. Pakistan had also re-joined by then. The next Games, in Kuala Lumpur, were the first held in Asia, and the first to include team sports, among them cricket and rugby sevens. The latter was won by New Zealand, for whom Jonah Lomu starred as they beat favourites Fiji.

In the new Millennium, the 2002 Games in Manchester became the largest sporting event staged in Britain, exceeding the 1948 Olympics, and set a new mark for the competition, especially in terms of its regeneration and legacy ambitions. Those in Melbourne four years later were dominated by the hosts, whose tally of 84 gold medals was as great as those of the next three nations.

The 2010 Games in Delhi were the costliest ever staged, with much of the budget of $11 billion spent on the spectacular opening ceremony. Four years later came the turn of Glasgow, where the sprinter Usain Bolt's prowess delighted the crowd. The subsequent Games, which took place in Queensland, were the first in the history of sport to have the same number of events for male and female competitors.

Jamaica's Usain Bolt celebrates winning gold in the 4x100 metres relay final at the 2014 Commonwealth Games in Glasgow.

After Birmingham, they will be held in Melbourne and then probably in Hamilton, Canada, in 2030, where they began a century earlier. They will continue to evolve – for instance, there has been debate recently about proposals to trim core events just to athletics and swimming to reduce costs.

There can be no doubt, however, that they have achieved their purpose of strengthening the bonds between competitors of different nations and have done so in an atmosphere of fellowship rarely found in what is now professional sport.

"Any of you who attended or watched the events of the Commonwealth Games," said the Queen after those of 1982 in Brisbane, "cannot have failed to notice the unique atmosphere of friendly rivalry and the generous applause for all the competitors.

"In a world more concerned with argument, disagreement and violence, the Games stand out as a demonstration of the better side of human nature and of the great value of the Commonwealth as an association of free and independent nations."

The Queen shares a laugh with athletes and Commonwealth Games officials in the dining hall of the Games village in Auckland, 1990.

At the Opening Ceremony for the 2014 Commonwealth Games at Celtic Park in Glasgow.

A NEW ORDER

1980s

THE WHOLE OF OURSELVES

Commonwealth visits in the 1980s

24–28 MAY 1980

The Queen visited Australia, fulfilling engagements in Canberra, Melbourne and Sydney.

26 SEPTEMBER–12 OCTOBER 1981

She returned to Australia the next year, visiting Perth and Adelaide as well as opening the CHOGM in Melbourne.

12–20 OCTOBER 1981

In New Zealand, the Queen went to Wellington, Auckland and Christchurch.

20–21 OCTOBER 1981

In Australia.

21–25 OCTOBER 1981

She also made a state visit to Sri Lanka.

15–18 APRIL 1982

The Queen was present at the Patriation Ceremony in Ottawa, which transferred full sovereignty to Canada.

5–13 OCTOBER 1982

The Queen travelled to Queensland, in Australia, for the Commonwealth Games.

13–14 OCTOBER 1982

From there, she made an extensive tour of the Pacific in Britannia, starting in Papua New Guinea.

18–23 OCTOBER 1982

She subsequently visited Solomon Islands, Nauru and Kiribati.

26–27 OCTOBER 1982

She and the Duke of Edinburgh were rowed ashore in war canoes at Tuvalu.

30 OCTOBER–1 NOVEMBER 1982

Fiji.

13–17 FEBRUARY 1983

The Queen visited Bermuda, Jamaica and Cayman Islands.

8–11 MARCH 1983

The Queen visited British Columbia, Canada.

9–10 NOVEMBER 1983

In Cyprus.

10–14 NOVEMBER 1983

A state visit was paid to Kenya.

14–17 NOVEMBER 1983

In Bangladesh.

17–26 NOVEMBER 1983

She visited India and attended the 7th CHOGM, hosted by Indira Gandhi.

25–26 MARCH 1984

Cyprus.

24 SEPTEMBER–7 OCTOBER 1984

A two-week tour of Canada included visits to Manitoba, Ontario and New Brunswick.

9–11 OCTOBER 1985

The Queen made her first visit to Belize, formerly British Honduras.

11–18 OCTOBER 1985

She went on to Nassau, in The Bahamas for the 8th CHOGM.

20 OCTOBER 1985

The Bahamas, Little Inagua Island (a private visit).

23 OCTOBER–3 NOVEMBER 1985

The Queen started the remainder of her Caribbean tour in Saint Kitts and Nevis, followed by Antigua and Barbuda, Dominica, Saint Lucia, Saint Vincent and the Grenadines, Barbados, Grenada and Trinidad and Tobago.

22 FEBRUARY–2 MARCH 1986

The Queen made a state visit to New Zealand, where she was met by demonstrators who threw eggs at her.

2–13 MARCH 1986

Australia, visiting New South Wales, Victoria and South Australia.

21–23 OCTOBER 1986

Hong Kong.

9–24 OCTOBER 1987

The Queen spent two weeks in Canada, attending the 10th CHOGM and visiting British Columbia, Saskatchewan and Quebec.

19 APRIL–10 MAY 1988

A three-week tour of Australia encompassed stops in Western Australia, Tasmania and Queensland, among many other engagements.

8–11 MARCH 1989

She visited the island of Barbados to mark the 350th anniversary of its Parliament.

9–11 OCTOBER 1989

Singapore.

9–11 OCTOBER 1989

She travelled to Malaysia for the 11th CHOGM.

In the Solomon Islands in 1982, during the South Pacific tour.

Until the 1980s, aside perhaps from The Beatles, the Queen had since her accession been the person that the rest of the world most associated with Britain. During that decade, however, two other women, each formidable in their own way, began to capture more of the media's attention – Margaret Thatcher and the Queen's daughter-in-law, Diana, the Princess of Wales.

This change in focus was perhaps inevitable over time, but its root causes and their consequences would test relations between Britain, the Queen and the Commonwealth. These still remained close, but the nature of a bond forged by a shared history began to be replaced by differing values which were not always so easily aligned.

The Queen continued to travel widely and regularly to Commonwealth countries, making more than 40 visits in the course of the decade. Among the most politically significant was that in November 1983 to India.

With Indira Gandhi at Rashtrapati Bhavan in India, 1983.

The Queen walks in a traditional Indian 'Palki' in Delhi, India, 1983.

Pilgrims disrupt Queen's schedule

A mass pilgrimage of Hindu revivalists forced a last-minute change in plans for the Queen's visit to Delhi yesterday. Soon after her arrival on a nine-day state visit, she was due to lay a wreath on the black marble memorial to Mahatma Gandhi, but security fears caused the ceremony to be postponed until today.

The Rajghat, where Gandhi's body was cremated on the banks of the holy river Yamuna, is one of the most sacred spots to Hindus, and yesterday Delhi was filled with the saffron flags and robes of the pilgrims, who are bearing pitchers of holy water across the country to whip up renewed commitment to the Hindu religion.

Swastika badges, gilded carts, and religious music mark the movement of the *yatra* or journey through the capital. The procession travelling by lorry and bus will take a month to make the trip from Hardwar north of here to the southernmost tip of India at Kanyakumari. Two other big *yatras* are also crossing the country, one from Katmandu to the south of Tamil Nadu, the other from Calcutta in the far east of the country to Somnath in the far west.

Mrs Gandhi has bitterly criticized the pilgrimages, organized by the Vishwa Hindu Parishad, the World Hindu Council, saying that they were perpetrating communal disharmony.

She said in a public speech that rabid communal forces, bent on dividing the country's unity, were behind the *Yatra*. She added that it would sow the seeds of distrust and sharpen the fears of the minority communities.

Hindu astrologers also managed to bring about a change in the Queen's programme. She was due to arrive at the ceremonial reception at Delhi airport promptly at noon, but this was judged on analysis of the augurics to be an inauspicious moment. Accordingly the British Airways Tristar in which the royal party is travelling taxied up to the red carpet at five minutes past instead.

The Queen was greeted at the foot of the aircraft steps by the President of India, Mr Giani Zail Singh, resplendent in a snowy white turban, his daughter Dr Gurdeep Kaur, and Mrs Gandhi.

She drove in a black bulletproof Mercedes – security precautions having been intensified here since the bomb explosion killed South Korean visitors in Burma – to the Rashtrapati Bhavan, the President's palace.

The route was decorated by 25ft high photographs of herself and the Duke of Edinburgh and arches of marigolds and jasmine spanned it. At the Rashtrapati Bhavan she called formally on the President, and in turn was called on by Mrs Gandhi.

At a glittering state banquet last night the Queen told guests that Britons were well placed to recognize India's contributions to world civilization, and she praised India's success in the "green revolution" and in space.

"We share a wealth of common values and common interests," she said. "A devotion to democratic ideals and to the institutions which maintain them, strong industrial and commercial links, and in Britain today a thriving community of people of Indian origin who make such a full contribution to our national life."

Earlier, as the Queen and Prince Philip left Dhaka on the way to Delhi there were further reminders of the Queen's moving visit on Wednesday to a Save The Children fund centre. She told the British Director, Mr Tony Hickmans: "I hope all goes well for your centre."

The Times, November 18, 1983

She was scheduled to land at Delhi airport at midday, but instead she arrived five minutes later after Hindu astrologers had declared that the original timing was inauspicious. As well as making a nine-day state visit, the Queen had come for the CHOGM, which was to be hosted by India's prime minister, Indira Gandhi.

Not everyone was, however, so welcoming. Demonstrators prevented her from laying a wreath at the shrine to Mahatma Gandhi, as she had done in 1961. This time, too, there was more vocal criticism of a lack of an apology for the massacre in 1919 at Amritsar by British troops of as many as 1,000 Indians who had been protesting against colonial detention laws.

Gamely, the Queen took in a tour of a factory in Hyderabad which made steam turbines. More to her fancy perhaps was the chance in New Delhi to go on one of the walkabouts which had become associated with her. Showing characteristic imperturbability, she did so while walking inside a traditional bridal palanquin, or "palki", borne by eight barefooted bearers.

At the banquet given in her honour, the Queen looked in her speech to the "wealth of common values and interests" that the two countries shared, not least the "thriving community of people of Indian origin who make such a full contribution to our national life."

In her Christmas speech that year, she again mentioned her visit to India. Her theme was how the revolution in speed of communications and travel was transforming the world. When her grandfather, George V, had visited India, she said, it had taken him three months to return. In less than that two-thirds of that time, she and the Duke of Edinburgh had visited eight countries that year, among them Jamaica, Kenya and Bangladesh.

Yet, she went on, "in spite of all the progress that has been made the greatest problem in the world today remains the gap between rich and poor countries." At the time, this was held by some commentators to be an overly political observation for the Queen to make. The truth of it, however, had been borne home during her travels in the sub-continent. Most memorably, while in Dhaka, in Bangladesh, she had taken the outstretched hand of a near-starving two-year-old who was being cared for by the charity Save the Children.

The Queen had discussed the challenges facing the poor of India with Mrs Gandhi. It was to be their last meeting. The following year, the premier was assassinated by two Sikhs of her own bodyguard. Their motivation was to avenge a military operation some months before by the Indian government – again at Amritsar – which had cost the lives of about 500 Sikh militants.

The world was changing apace, as the Queen had noted, but in 1982 she and Prince Philip received a timeless welcome to the Pacific island of Tuvalu. They were rowed ashore from Britannia in war canoes. Then the monarch was carried aloft in another canoe on the shoulders of garlanded islanders to the meeting house in Funafuti. The Duke followed behind in similar style.

The first tour by a British monarch to what had once been called the Ellice Islands also took in stops in Fiji, Kiribati, Nauru, the Solomon Islands and Papua New Guinea. The Queen appeared to have a particularly close connection to Polynesia's peoples, and on a visit to New Zealand the previous year, she had been met with a greeting given to few – *Te kotuku rarenga tahi* ("Welcome rare white heron of singular flight").

The Queen is rowed ashore by islanders from Tuvalu as she sits in a decorated dug-out canoe, 1982.

The Queen and Prince Philip are carried down Main Street by Tuvaluans in traditional dress in 1982.

Magical welcome for the Queen in Tuvalu

The Queen, in 30 years on the throne, can rarely have experienced a welcome like it. Her greeting yesterday on the South Pacific islands of Tuvalu, formerly the Ellice Islands, was almost beyond the imagination and she visibly enjoyed every moment of it.

Family and friends who knew the island of Funafuti could have told her, but until the Queen sailed to the island on board the motor vessel Activity, she could not have imagined the wonderful greeting that awaited her.

Far in the distance she could see the thin line of red, white and blue dugout canoes around the two special craft that waited in the shallows to take her and the Duke of Edinburgh ashore.

As she approached, the islanders' haunting words of welcome wafted over the waves. They raised their paddles and ceremonial fishing rods in salute.

The Queen stepped into her canoe, painted in the Tuvaluan colours of gold and turquoise, picking her way through the mass of foliage and decoration that covered the seat.

Ahead of her was a garlanded welcoming committee, some with Union Flags stuck into their headbands. The only incongruous note was struck by Mr Neal Davidson, the Attorney-General, who arrived in pinstripe suit, stiff collar, wig and gown.

The Queen looked somewhat apprehensive as her craft was lifted gently from the sea and slowly raised on to the shoulders of 26 burly islanders. She was carried head and shoulders above the crowds as her bearers walked up the pebble beach to the sandy lane that led the 200 yards to the meeting house. Island girls began dancing and choirs sang. The Queen laughed and waved.

Once at the meeting house the official welcome took place in which Dr Tomasi Puapua, the Prime Minister, recalled the Duke's promise in 1959 to bring the Queen with him next time he called at the island.

Then scores of dancers rose in turn to honour the Queen. One member of the official party, Mr Henry Naisali, the Finance Minister, could not resist joining in and leapt from his seat to join the dancers.

During the welcoming ceremony the royal couple were presented with exotic necklaces of mother of pearl which are supposed to bring good luck.

After a reception on the Royal Yacht Britannia, the Queen again went ashore for a South Sea island feast.

The Times, October 27, 1982

The Queen is crowned with a headdress of frangipani flowers in Tuvalu.

Drinking from a coconut in Tuvalu.

The Queen and Prince Philip receive gifts while watching traditional dancers in Tuvalu, 1982.

Her next journey to Polynesia, in 1986, attracted more controversy. In New Zealand, Maori protests about the Treaty of Waitangi, by signing which their ancestors had ceded sovereignty to Queen Victoria, were starting to gather momentum. When Queen Elizabeth was passing Ellerslie racecourse, demonstrators threw eggs at her car. One hit her and left a mark on her coat. Although somewhat shocked, she would later joke that she preferred to have her eggs at breakfast.

More incidents continued to mar the tour, culminating in that in which several women bared their backsides to the Queen – a traditional Maori insult. It was a reminder that for all the Queen wanted to emphasise the future of her realms, and the ties that might unite them, for some of their citizens there was a reckoning to be had first with the past.

It was Britain's perception of the importance of those ties which led in 1982 to it retaking the Falkland Islands after they had been occupied by Argentine forces. The outcome of the war boosted the standing at home of Mrs Thatcher, and internationally of Britain.

This would arguably become a factor later in the decade as the Queen sought to preserve the delicate equilibrium of the Commonwealth. Of more immediate concern to her, however, was an invasion of another of her realms, Grenada.

After the Caribbean island had won independence in 1974, it had retained the Queen as its head of state, and it was a member of the Commonwealth. A Marxist government led by Maurice Bishop took power in a coup in 1979, but in 1983 he was deposed in turn by soldiers loyal to his deputy and then executed.

Fearful that these events would presage closer relations between Grenada and the Communist bloc – Cuban labourers were already building an airstrip on the island – the US government of Ronald Reagan invaded Grenada. Although the conspirators were routed, the operation was launched without meaningful advance notice being given to Britain.

The Queen was reported to be particularly irate, despite the close relationship that she and Reagan came to enjoy. Nevertheless, the Americans soon departed and anger subsided.

Australia
independent at last

The Queen yesterday left traditional Maori insults and political brouhaha in New Zealand and arrived in Canberra for a 12-day visit which, for all Australia's reputation for belligerent egalitarianism, is unlikely to be touched by the same kind of controversy.

Her first official duty was to grant Australians the full independence from Britain which many thought they had decades ago.

In a simple ceremony at Government House here, attended by Mr Bob Hawke, the Prime Minister, and his Cabinet, the Queen signed a proclamation activating from today the Australia Acts of 1986, recently passed by the British and Federal Parliaments.

The Acts remove the residual – and by general agreement outdated – legislative, executive and judicial fetters which could be imposed from Britain.

The unhanding by Australia of such control has been a process which started with the effective granting of self-government in 1901 – when colonies like Victoria and New South Wales federated as a nation – and continued through the 1930s but which is only now complete.

The final phase, which started more than a decade ago, was delayed as much by a certain weariness in various state parliaments at the prospect of losing further authority to Canberra as by reluctance in Westminster to approve it.

The most significant change in practical terms is abolition of the right of appeal to the Privy Council. The view has been widely held in legal circles for years here that it was intolerable for a foreign body to have overriding legal jurisdiction in Australia, and henceforth the High Court is the final judicial authority.

The Act also scraps powers which British governments have in theory retained but in effect not exercised for years, as a link between state governments in Australia and the Crown.

The New Zealand tour was incident-filled to the end. On Saturday three women in their early twenties exposed their buttocks to the Queen as she was being driven to a garden party in Christchurch.

The *Whakapohane*, as this traditional Maori gesture is known, was clearly seen by the Queen, and was the second time on the tour that she and the Duke of Edinburgh had been confronted by protesters in this way. She was also hit by an egg thrown by a young woman and encountered a number of demonstrations.

For all the attention these protests have attracted, it would be a mistake to imagine that New Zealand – arguably the most ardently royalist of all Commonwealth countries – has undergone some dramatic metamorphosis. The demonstrators were invariably in small groups and generally representative of fringe political groups.

Mr David Lange, the Prime Minister, clearly testy at the coverage the incidents have attracted in the British media, said to British journalists on Saturday: "She is the Queen of New Zealand. I don't remember complaining when a man got into her bedroom at Buckingham Palace. I wish you people would look after her as well as we do in New Zealand".

The Times, March 3, 1986

Her coat spattered by an egg, the Queen looks pensive in New Zealand in 1986.

After the turmoil of her own visit, the Queen meets members of the touring New Zealand cricket team, and the England players, at Lord's Cricket Ground in 1986.

It was not often that The Queen was discomfited by political change and upheavals in Commonwealth countries of which she was also head of state. Even if she felt saddened by turns of events, she was pragmatic about the scope of her ability to influence them. For instance, in 1987, a series of coups in Fiji left the military in charge, despite its Governor-General and Buckingham Palace encouraging them to return to democracy.

When Colonel Sitiveni Rabuka's regime announced that Fiji would become a republic, the Queen accepted the practicalities of the situation, although she had hoped that the nation's people might have been allowed a say in the matter. Fiji was deemed to have left the Commonwealth, but it would rejoin it 10 years later.

The British government had taken a somewhat less emollient view of the situation in Fiji and the episode demonstrated that it did not always march in step with the Palace. This was not surprising given the different cultures prevailing there and in Downing Street, but there had been a more serious crisis the year before when an article in *The Sunday Times* claimed that the Queen found Mrs Thatcher "uncaring."

Its publication was a reflection of a media now much less deferential than even a decade before, and one which began to treat the Royal Family – most obviously the Princess of Wales – as celebrities ripe for scrutiny.

The source for the report turned out to be the Queen's press secretary, Michael Shea, who was ultimately portrayed as having claimed too much knowledge of the monarch's well-guarded views. Nonetheless, there was little doubt that she was especially troubled by one of the examples he cited, namely the prime minister's disinclination, for economic reasons, to impose sanctions on South Africa so as to pressure it into reform.

The issue promised to split the Commonwealth. The 1985 CHOGM in Nassau had been witness to much ill-feeling, again smoothed over at the Queen's promptings. Nevertheless, the following year 32 nations, mostly from Africa and the West Indies, boycotted the Commonwealth Games in Edinburgh in protest at the lack of action by Britain.

It was in this context that, directly after the Games ended in early August 1986, the leaders of six leading Commonwealth nations attended a summit with Mrs Thatcher in London to discuss South Africa. The night before, they met for a dinner at Buckingham Palace hosted by the Queen.

At the end of the conference, Mrs Thatcher did not sign up for sanctions, as the other heads of government did, but she did show some movement, announcing bans on investment and the promotion of tourism.

Peace of a sorts returned to the Commonwealth, an achievement ascribed by its Secretary-General, Sir Sonny Ramphal, to the Queen's interventions at the dinner. The head of the Commonwealth had, he said, gone "the extra mile" to restore harmony to the organisation. Even if grave troubles lay ahead for the Queen herself, her family of nations still looked to her to rise above their own.

(Standing left to right) Rajiv Gandhi, Brian Mulroney, S.S. Ramphal, Robert Hawke and Robert Mugabe; (seated left to right) Margaret Thatcher, Lynden Pindling and Kenneth Kaunda meet to discuss South Africa, 1986.

The Queen at the 8th CHOGM in Nassau, The Bahamas, 1985.

PAST AND PRESENT

1990s

THE SHOULDERS OF OUR ELDERS

Commonwealth visits in the 1990s

1–16 FEBRUARY 1990

A state visit to New Zealand lasting two weeks took in the Commonwealth Games and the commemoration of the 150th anniversary of the signing with the Maori peoples of the Treaty of Waitangi.

27 JUNE–1 JULY 1990

The Queen made a short visit to Alberta, Ontario and Quebec in Canada.

7 OCTOBER 1991

Kenya (an overnight stop).

8–10 OCTOBER 1991

Namibia.

10–15 OCTOBER 1991

The Queen attended the 12th CHOGM in Harare, Zimbabwe.

18–25 FEBRUARY 1992

A visit to Australia marked the sesqui-centenary of the foundation of the city of Sydney.

28–30 MAY 1992

Malta.

30 JUNE–2 JULY 1992

The Queen celebrated the 125th anniversary of Confederation in Canada.

18–24 OCTOBER 1993

The 13th CHOGM was staged in Cyprus, with a reception held aboard Britannia.

18 FEBRUARY–8 MARCH 1994

Beginning in Anguilla, the Queen and Prince Philip made a three-week tour of the Caribbean aboard Britannia, in the course of which the royal yacht sailed its one millionth mile. During this tour, they visited Dominica, Guyana, Belize, Cayman Islands, Jamaica and The Bahamas.

8–10 MARCH 1994

Bermuda.

13–22 AUGUST 1994

Canada (Nova Scotia, British Columbia and Northwest Territories).

19–25 MARCH 1995

For the first time in half a century, the Queen paid a state visit to South Africa, where she was hosted by President Nelson Mandela.

30 OCTOBER–11 NOVEMBER 1995

The Queen attended the 14th CHOGM in Auckland, New Zealand.

23 JUNE–2 JULY 1997

The Queen visited Newfoundland and Ontario in Canada.

6–12 OCTOBER 1997

She visited Pakistan, a month after the funeral of Diana, Princess of Wales.

12–18 OCTOBER 1997

In India.

17–23 SEPTEMBER 1998

The Queen spent four days in Brunei, then departed for Malaysia, which hosted Asia's first Commonwealth Games, in Kuala Lumpur.

7–9 NOVEMBER 1999

The Queen visited Ghana and addressed its Parliament.

9–15 NOVEMBER 1999

She attended the 16th CHOGM in South Africa, before heading to Mozambique.

As the Queen reached her seventies, her programme of tours became less extensive, even if still taxing at an age when most of her generation was already taking life easier. On average, each year during the 1990s she travelled to one Commonwealth nation or region, often timing her visit to coincide with that year's CHOGM.

There were other changes, too, though these were not of her making. Events such as the unexpected collapse of the Soviet bloc in the final days of the previous decade reframed the world, as did the release from prison in 1990 of Nelson Mandela. In London, a political era came to an end the same year with the departure from Downing Street of Margaret Thatcher.

The domestic popularity of the Royal Family, meanwhile, was tested as never before during the Queen's reign. The spotlight that fell on the failing marriages of Prince Charles and Prince Andrew led to revelations which divided opinion in Britain. This process of reappraisal culminated in the public reaction to the death in 1997 of Diana, Princess of Wales, one which was at times critical of the Queen herself.

Abroad, however, her standing remained undiminished, and from 1991 the Commonwealth as an organisation began formally to acknowledge the key role that she often played in its deliberations.

The fortieth anniversary of her accession that year was marked by the commissioning of an 18-carat gold mace, decorated with rubies and with enamel flags representing the 52 member states. It was used thereafter at ceremonies such as Commonwealth Day. Since the Queen did not always attend these events in person, the mace became a symbol of her presence, and so of how important was thought her ability to unify the disparate states.

The Commonwealth was at something of a low ebb as the decade began. It had been riven by disagreements over South Africa and had played little part in influencing the end of the Cold War. Yet, given its lead by the Queen, it simply kept on doing its job, and emerged from the nineties in rather better shape.

Whatever the organisation's internal divisions, that membership was viewed as conferring advantages was confirmed by Mozambique's application to join it. The country had no historic ties to Britain – it had been a Portuguese colony – but it was admitted in 1995, as was Cameroon. Consideration of the terms on which other countries might join then led to an important declaration: that applicants should recognise the British monarch as head of the Commonwealth.

Although only an implication, this was the first time that the organisation had in effect stated that the position was tied to the British throne and was therefore hereditary. More explicit was the decision in 1997 by the Secretary-General, Chief Emeka Anyaoku, a Nigerian diplomat and former foreign minister, to invite the Queen to open the CHOGM being held in Edinburgh.

Until then, her participation in the work of the conference had in theory been kept to the fringes. From now on, there could be no doubt how close this was to her heart. Increasingly perhaps, she saw it as forming a major part of her legacy.

The Queen with Prime Minister Tony Blair and heads of state at the 15th CHOGM in Edinburgh, 1977.

An old friend, familiar to many in the Commonwealth, would, however, not be handed on. By 1994, the government of John Major was under pressure to save money. With royal finances under scrutiny following the announcement that the Queen would pay tax like everyone else, it was agreed that Britannia would be decommissioned.

The decision was confirmed in 1997 by the incoming administration of Tony Blair. In the interim, there had been time for a farewell in harness for a ship that, over 45 years of service, had come to feel like home for the Queen.

In 1994, she and Prince Philip toured the West Indies aboard Britannia for three weeks, visiting islands and former realms that included Anguilla, Guyana, Dominica and Jamaica. During the voyage, the royal yacht sailed its one millionth nautical mile, an achievement celebrated by the Queen with the cutting of a cake.

It did duty for the last time at the ceremony in June 1997 in which, under the pouring rain, Hong Kong was handed back to China. Blair's press secretary, Alastair Campbell, later revealed that, having seen there at first hand the soft power that the yacht projected, the prime minister realised that a mistake had been made. Yet the political cost of reversing it made that impossible.

The Queen was still capable, however, of forging new friendships. The end of Nelson Mandela's captivity after 27 years, and the subsequent ending of apartheid in South Africa, caused something of an identity crisis for the Commonwealth. It deprived the organisation of one of the few issues around which a majority of its members could rally.

Nevertheless, from their first meeting at the CHOGM in Harare in 1991, the Queen and Mandela enjoyed a delight in each other's company rare in such circles. Mandela had only been invited as an observer, and it was the Queen's decision to invite him to the formal banquet.

He told her with a courtly twinkle that she was looking good despite her busy schedule. She replied that that might not be the case tomorrow, after she had taken 16 meetings, adding mischievously that someone had asked her if she had been to Africa before. She thought she had seen more of Africa than almost anyone else.

The Queen and Prince Philip walk with South African President Nelson Mandela in Cape Town, 1995.

The Queen arrives at Durban airport in South Africa in 1995. Earlier, at a function in Pretoria, she was named Motlalepula – "She who brings the rain".

By the following year, such was the understanding between them that Mandela felt able to compliment the Queen on having lost weight, and he was one of the very few people to address her as "Elizabeth".

So it was that in 1995, with South Africa having re-joined the Commonwealth and Mandela now its president, the Queen returned to the country for the first time in 48 years. The last time that she visited had been with her parents and her sister, on the tour during which she had marked her twenty-first birthday with a pledge to dedicate her life to serving the "British family of nations" – the Commonwealth.

In those days, the Royal Family had sailed all the way from Britain on a battleship and had stayed in southern Africa for more than two months. Although on this occasion she was to be there for less than a week, the Queen echoed her earlier manner of arrival by steaming into Table Bay aboard Britannia – albeit having flown in first on a commercial airliner.

Her officials said that for her the visit ranked on a par with those to Russia and to China, and she would later describe it as one of the great experiences of her life. More than a quarter of a million people turned out to see her, with Black and White shoulders rubbing together in the crowd in a way unthinkable only a few years before.

The tour heralded the best rainy season for a decade and the country's deputy president, Thabo Mbeki, subsequently bestowed a new title on the Queen – Motlalepula, "She who brings the rain".

Queen welcomed by Mandela as thousands cheer

In a rare display of post-imperial splendour, the Royal Yacht Britannia nosed into Cape Town harbour yesterday as the Queen began her state visit to South Africa.

On a brilliant morning under Table Mountain, capped with its tablecloth of cloud, and accompanied by a flotilla of small craft laden to the gunwales with sightseers, the yacht sailed close to the notorious Robben Island, the prison that was home to President Mandela for so many years.

A predominantly White crowd of thousands packed every ledge of the quayside, with only a sprinkling of Black faces, apart from a few well-drilled platoons of schoolchildren. Even in the new South Africa, the five rands (£1) bus fare from the Black townships is money that can be better spent. As the Queen descended the gangway, the warm southeasterly breeze that freshened the air, and is therefore known locally as the Cape Doctor, snatched at the Queen's blue straw hat. She had to keep one cautious hand fixed to her head as Mr Mandela stepped forward to greet her with a hearty: "Your Majesty, welcome to South Africa." With equal joviality he greeted the Duke of Edinburgh with: "Your Royal Highness, how are you?"

As a South African navy band played one British and two South African national anthems – the new one and the old Afrikaner one – competing royalty displayed a clash of colour on the jetty. The Queen wore a sky blue linen coat; Rochelle Mtirara, a niece of Mr Mandela who now acts as his presidential lady, wore the brilliant orange dress and headgear of a member of the royal house of the Thembu tribe, of which Mr Mandela is a prominent member.

Ships' klaxons blared, the crowd applauded and cheered, and six jet fighters roared overhead in formation trailing red, white and blue smoke as the Queen met a line-up of leading public figures including Archbishop Desmond Tutu.

At the presidential residence in Cape Town, the Queen presented Mr Mandela with the insignia of the Order of Merit, of which the only other living foreign recipient is Mother Teresa. Mr Mandela invested her with South Africa's Order of Good Hope.

The Queen presented an annual scholarship for a South African graduate to study at the London School of Economics, and a blue leather desk set. She received in return a brooch of precious stones set in the design and colour of the new South African flag. It contained everything but diamonds, one of the country's leading exports. But the Queen already owns the biggest one ever mined in South Africa: the Cullinan, presented to Edward VII.

At a state banquet last night, the Queen came as close as she is likely to during her tour to satisfying Afrikaner demands for an apology for their treatment at British hands during the Boer War. "Only eight years after our two countries had been at war, with all the pain and suffering which that entailed, especially for the Afrikaner people, Queen Victoria's son, the Duke of Connaught, laid the foundation stone of the Union Building in Pretoria," she said.

Mr Mandela accepted an invitation to make a return state visit to Britain next year.

The Times, March 21, 1995

The Queen and President Mandela attend a service to mark Human Rights Day.

With President Mandela at a banquet in Cape Town, South Africa, 1997.

On a walkabout in Durban, South Africa.

The Queen meeting children during her walkabout with Nceba Faku,
the first Black mayor of Port Elizabeth, South Africa, 1997.

Success such as this perhaps offered the Queen some relief from the buffeting that the Royal Family was suffering at home, where the disastrous fire at Windsor Castle in 1992 was only one of numerous shocks that she stoically endured. Yet not all her travels were trouble-free.

Her reception for the heads of state at the 1993 CHOGM in Cyprus – held aboard the royal yacht – was reported to have been exceptionally enjoyable, with the Queen and her guests, many of whom she had known for years, in a knockabout mood even during her speech.

She had earlier been noisily jeered, however, in Nicosia by a crowd of Greek Cypriots. They wanted an apology for the execution of nine Eoka guerrillas during the armed uprising in the late 1950s against Britain's control of the island.

The cost of the Empire resurfaced again during the Queen's state visit in October 1997 to Pakistan and India. This was a tour, long in the planning, that was intended to mark the fiftieth anniversary of India's independence. Yet it was inevitably overshadowed by the death of Diana shortly before and, as it got underway, by some unguarded remarks in Islamabad by the Foreign Secretary, Robin Cook. He said that Britain stood ready to mediate in the conflict between Pakistan and India for control of Kashmir.

Since this reflected Pakistan's negotiating stance, the Indian government was angered even before the Queen arrived. There were then further rows over protocol at a banquet in Madras and after members of the royal party were manhandled by police at the city's airport.

All this detracted from the significance of the Queen's visit to Amritsar, where she laid a wreath at the site of the massacre of protestors by British troops in 1919. She made no formal apology (and Prince Philip queried the number of the dead inscribed on a plaque), but her gesture was widely viewed in India as, if not an act of contrition, then certainly as one of conciliation.

The Queen found herself amidst more trouble the following year, when she travelled to Malaysia, which was hosting the Commonwealth Games. Its long-serving prime minister, Mahathir Mohamad, had accused his former deputy, Anwar Ibrahim, a potential political rival, of a series of scandalous offences.

As the Queen attended a service at St Mary's cathedral in Kuala Lumpur, thousands of Ibrahim's supporters massed at a rally nearby. The mood was such that when her convoy passed it attracted 'boos', and the Queen then found herself in the invidious position of making a call on Mohamad as Ibrahim was detained and the meeting broken up by riot police.

If there was at last a turning point in the monarchy's fortunes during the decade, it was the result in November 1999 of Australia's referendum on becoming a republic. The Queen was still personally popular there, as for instance was shown by the crowds who greeted her visit in 1992.

Receiving flowers from the crowd outside Sydney Town Hall, 1992.

Australia's royalists put flags out for the Queen

"There's Queenie. Lovely old dear!" came a whooping cry from the crowd as the Queen and the Duke of Edinburgh emerged from their jumbo jet at Sydney's international airport yesterday evening.

The uncommonly intimate and somewhat raucous greeting prompted a momentary arching of the royal eyebrows, but there were also graceful smiles and waves for the crowd of thousands who had waited hours in sweltering heat for the sovereign.

The royal couple are in Australia for a seven-day visit to mark the 150th anniversary of the founding of Sydney and to meet Paul Keating, the prime minister.

The Queen, in a snappy tomato-red suit and hat, had the local police on their toes within minutes as she ventured out to shake hands with flag-waving admirers and accept bunches of flowers. Two women struggled to hold a large "We love you, Liz!" banner, which was billowing in the hot wind like a spinnaker, while a cluster of burnished young surfers bounced up and down like pogo sticks, their enthusiastic cheers merging into one long sustained "Yeah!" as the Queen walked coolly past.

"I think she's just terrific. My grandmother taught me to curtsy in case I ever got to meet the Queen," said Teresa Bennett, whose energetic curtsies went unnoticed. "She's just as much our Queen as yours," announced Liang Li, proudly waving his Australian flag as the Queen's Rolls Royce rolled past. Mr Li was born in China, moved to Hong Kong 20 years ago and emigrated to Australia in 1989.

The Queen's visit comes just as the public debate is hotting up. Last month, Mr Keating proposed that Australia drop the Union Jack from the corner of its national flag, leaving the stars of the Southern Cross. Some have called for the inclusion of a kangaroo on the flag.

A number of republican lobby groups have emerged in the past year, including the Australian Republican Movement founded by the former cricket captain Ian Chappell and Malcolm Turnbull, the lawyer who defended Peter Wright in the Spycatcher case. The movement claims that between 42 and 44 per cent of Australians support the idea of a republic, against between 55 and 56 per cent who support a monarchy. They want a referendum on the subject by 2001.

On her tour of Sydney, Dubbo, Canberra and Adelaide, the Queen will no doubt be shielded from the controversy. She will devote much of her time to meeting thousands of schoolchildren. But, whatever her reception, there is little doubt that she will divide Australia on this visit.

The Times, February 19, 1992

The Queen receives an enthusiastic welcome in Nauru, then part of Australia, in 1982.

The republican movement had been growing steadily, however, backed by much of the local media and the government of Paul Keating. His successor, John Howard, backed the monarchy, but felt obliged to put the issue to the vote. It came as something of a surprise when the result showed a strong preference to retain the Queen, although this may have owed not a little to the proposed alternative, a president nominated by politicians.

The next day, the Queen left Britain for the CHOGM in South Africa. She stopped first in Ghana. On her last visit, in 1961, she had made headlines dancing with Kwame Nkrumah. The president now was Jerry Rawlings. He had twice attained power via coups but had since served two terms after winning elections.

Under the country's constitution, Rawlings was due to step down shortly, yet there were worries that he might cling to office. The British government's view of the purpose of the Queen's visit, as one official told *The Times*, was that it should encourage him to stay the course.

"We want to demonstrate to other states on the continent that the more they behave themselves at home, the more they are likely to attract foreign help." To that end, the Queen's speech to Ghana's parliament did not beat about the bush.

It reminded its audience that Rawlings, who was sitting beside her, would soon be expected to return to civilian life. This prompted loud shouts from the president's supporters but, once the hubbub had died down, the Queen continued, emphasising the need for fair elections and the maintenance of rights such as freedom of speech.

Rawlings duly went without a fuss. Its detractors might think that monarchy was outdated, but as the Queen often demonstrated, there were still times and places where she could achieve results with more ease than politicians, where her word remained sovereign.

The Queen meets the President of Ghana, Flight Lieutenant Jerry Rawlings, at Accra Airport, 1999.

Your Good Health: attending a state banquet in Accra, Ghana, in 1999.

At a traditional Durbar gathering of tribal chiefs during the Queen's visit to Accra, Ghana, in 1999.

Queen is hailed in tribal welcome

Thirteen tribal chiefs and six queen mothers greeted the Queen on the first full day of her state visit to Ghana yesterday. This was what royal tours must have been like in the old colonial days: a durbar at which lesser chiefs paid homage to the Great White Chief from across the sea on a dusty parade ground under a merciless sky, accompanied by marathons of native dancing and the piercing thunder of drums the size of oil tankers.

Tribal chieftaincy remains a vital cultural thread in modern Ghana, and their first opportunity to welcome the Queen since 1961 was a well-attended celebration. The only notable absentee was Nana Osei Tutu II, chief of the Ashanti, the country's largest ethnic group. His official apology for absence pleaded court mourning for his recently deceased predecessor, but he was rumoured to have taken umbrage at not being given first place in the presentation line-up.

Others made up for him with their exotic dress and titles. Here was the Omanhene of Prang (a mathematics teacher when he is not enstooled), there Odeefuo Boa Amponsem III (John Appiah, a retired public administrator). And there, among the lesser chiefs, Dr Oti Boateng, who claims to be a cousin of the current Home Office Minister.

Under their parasols of red and gold, purple and blue, the chiefs lined up to meet the Queen, herself shielded from a sun boiling the air at nearly 100F by a parasol 8ft in diameter. She managed to look cool in a multicoloured spotted dress that was far less showy than the cotton dresses of the dancing troupe printed with side-by-side portraits of the Queen and President Jerry Rawlings, her host.

During a drive around Accra Ghanaians lined the route six deep, but when so many of the young ones are in scout or Sunday school uniform, the suspicion lingers that they were not there entirely of their own free will.

In a spiky address to the 200 members of the Ghanaian Parliament in the modern horseshoe chamber more akin to Edinburgh than Westminster, the Queen plainly voiced her Government's desire to see improvements in Ghana's imperfect democracy.

"Next year your President, who has led you through momentous changes, will reach the end of his second term," said the Queen, suddenly halted in mid-flow by a noisy outburst of laughter and cheering from the opposition benches. She eventually continued: "His successor is to be chosen freely and fairly by the people of Ghana. This election will itself demonstrate the political change and freedom which Ghana now enjoys."

Then she got to the sting. "An open society, a free media, a truly independent judiciary and a democratically chosen, accountable executive provide the conditions under which the equality of opportunity, initiative and a stable society can flourish." Those are the very areas in which Britain feels Ghana still falls short of the best democratic standards.

But the Queen sweetened the pill by making a complimentary reference to Britain's 200,000 citizens of Ghanaian descent, including one of her ministers, although she did not refer to Paul Boateng by name.

At an exchange of gifts in the improbable surroundings of Christianbourg Castle, built by the Danes for their 17th-century slave trade, President Rawlings gave the Queen a bronze statue of a horse.

She countered with an inlaid Linley sycamore box. "I've brought a box made by my nephew, David. He's very good at making things out of wood; he's a very good designer, you know." How the carmakers and whisky distillers of Britain must wish they had that particular sales rep on their books.

The Times, November 9, 1999

The Queen visits schoolchildren at the Wireless Cluster Junior School in Accra, Ghana, in 1999.

The company of HMS Bulwark, a Royal Navy amphibious assault ship, salute the Queen at Grand Harbour, Valletta, in 2015.

For many, the turn of the millennium prompted contemplation of the future. In the glib phrase associated with Britain's government of the day, for the Queen and the monarchy "things could only get better". What was perhaps unexpected was that they did.

With the deaths of Diana, Princess of Wales, and then in 2002 of Queen Elizabeth, the Queen Mother, and the Queen's sister, Princess Margaret, the sovereign herself was liberated from the long shadows cast by those whose personalities had naturally drawn more of the spotlight.

The acclaim she received from the British public during her Golden Jubilee celebrations, which also occurred in 2002, confirmed that any dip in her own popularity had been only temporary. Over the next decade, many of the other difficulties that had dogged the Queen also resolved themselves. The Prince of Wales, for instance, remarried happily, while Prince William and his wife, Catherine, increasingly shared the burden of royal duties.

As the Queen neared 80, her own way of doing things seemed vindicated, and the influence that her example wielded without equal. By contrast, the Commonwealth still appeared to be seeking a mission, and was more than ever in need of her to guide it.

Yet, with age, although she still attended the Heads of Government meetings held every two years, the Queen began to be seen less frequently in person by its peoples. When she did travel, it was often to those Commonwealth nations of which she had the strongest memories and to which she had the deepest ties.

In 2000, she made another memorable tour of Australia, the first of three visits in six years – a third of all her trips to Commonwealth countries in that time. It was her first journey to the country since the referendum and, while the welcome was as warm as ever, Palace officials made it clear that the Queen accepted that republican tendencies were still strong.

Even so, one of the highlights of her tour was a visit to Bourke, a town in the New South Wales bush whose name is synonymous in Australian slang with "the middle of nowhere". Still more remote was the community of Coolabah – "Two stores and a pub, mate," one inhabitant told *The Times* – some 80 miles further on.

Coolabah held, however, the distinction of having returned the highest percentage vote in Australia in favour of retaining the monarchy. When the Queen came to Bourke, the entire town of Coolabah went to see her. Or at least 46 of its 50 citizens did so, by bus. Those who had voted the other way stayed at home.

The Times witnessed the ensuing encounter. "'We voted 92 percent for you,' said Marie Norris, proudly, as she pressed a rose into the royal glove. 'I know,' replied the Queen. 'You've come specially today, have you?' 'Yes,' they chorused, raising cameras in unison to capture the historic moment. 'Within half a minute, the Queen of Coolabah and All Australia had moved on.'"

The delegation, meanwhile, returned to Coolabah to celebrate with a goat race – "doubtless a local tradition." The Queen would come back to Australia in 2002 for the CHOGM, and then four years later for the Commonwealth Games.

Then in 2011, she and Prince Philip went to Perth for that year's CHOGM. As the summit also brought together many of the Queen's realms, it was used by the Palace and Downing Street as an opportunity to get those nations to agree to reforms to the outdated laws governing royal marriages and the succession. For instance, the next heir, and perhaps one day the Commonwealth's leader, would henceforth be Prince William's firstborn child, not the eldest male.

The main business of the CHOGM itself was the release of a report containing more than 100 recommendations for the future of the Commonwealth. Many of these, such as the creation of a commissioner for human rights, divided the organisation, leaving it seeming more than ever unified only by its allegiance to the Queen.

For her part, in her speech to the meeting she openly encouraged the Commonwealth's more hidebound members to adopt a bolder, more liberal approach to the future. The unspoken issue which preoccupied her hosts, however, was whether, as seemed probable at 85, this sixteenth visit to Australia would prove to be her last. If so, she had created enough memories to last a lifetime.

(Left to right) Bangladesh Prime Minister Sheikh Hasina, the Queen, Australia Prime Minister Julia Gillard, and Trinidad and Tobago Prime Minister Kamla Persad-Bissessar pose for the official female heads of state photo at the 22nd CHOGM in Perth, Australia, in 2011.

For the 16th time
(and don't dare say it's the last)
Australia says: 'G'day your Maj'

As the Queen arrived in Australia yesterday, stepping off the plane and getting straight down to business as if jet lag were an affliction of ordinary mortals, not sovereigns, the question on everyone's lips was one that no one would be so foolish as to voice in her presence: would this be her last trip Down Under?

Her tour with the Duke of Edinburgh, a curtain raiser to the Commonwealth Heads of Government Meeting in Perth next week, is the Queen's 16th visit to Australia since 1954. With the Queen aged 85 and the Duke 90, there has been much speculation, some of it fanned by sources inside Buckingham Palace, that this will be the last time that she undertakes the exhausting journey to the other side of the world.

By the time another visit would be due, she would probably be 90 and the Duke would find it hard to cope with such an arduous journey. Would the Queen, who has never done a trip of any significance without him, go by herself? Possibly not. But the official line is that this is not being billed as her last time in Australia.

They would, it is true, say that anyway, on the ground that it might not go down well here to announce "That's all, folks" on behalf of the Queen. It is also true that it is never wise to underestimate the Queen's sense of duty. She has a great fondness for Australia, and regards her job as one that comes without a retirement plan: if she has breath in her body, and can make it up the steps of the plane, then perhaps no one should rule out the possibility of another tour in a few years.

As she arrived in Canberra, walking down the steps of the

chartered BA flight that took her on the 22-hour flight from London, neither the Queen nor the Duke betrayed any signs of being worn out by their journey. To judge by her smile, the Queen, in an aqua Stewart Parvin coat, seemed delighted to be here. On the airstrip she was given a bouquet by Margaret Cunningham, 64, who as a six-year-old had presented her with a bunch of flowers in Canberra on the 1954 tour.

Ms Cunningham, a retired art teacher now living in Bateau Bay, New South Wales, said: "I said it was lovely to see her again after all these years. There was a glint in her eye. She looked at me with those same blue eyes from all those years ago, they never change a steady warm gaze, honest and sincere."

Even if the pace of this tour is not quite as frenetic as in years gone by, there is no sense that the Queen is taking it easy, or is not up to the job. After the ceremonial welcome in Canberra last night she goes straight into a full diary of engagements today with an audience with the Governor-General, Quentin Bryce – who, despite the name and the title, is a woman – and a visit to a flower show. There are two dozen engagements in 11 days, a more than reasonable workload for a woman who is a quarter of a century past the normal retirement age.

If the crowds during this visit fail to match those of 1954, the Queen can console herself with the thought that most Australians still want her as their head of state. Twelve years after the republican movement lost the referendum to change the Constitution, there is no credible political momentum behind the campaign to get rid of the monarchy. An opinion poll yesterday showed that support for the monarchy, at 55 per cent, was at its highest since 1991. Only 34 per cent of Australians want a republic.

Most republicans concede that the Queen will get a warm welcome. "There has never been anything other than respect and affection for the Queen," said Malcolm Turnbull, a prominent republican and former opposition leader. "I think all Australians, republicans or not, welcome the Queen's visit."

The Times, October 20, 2011

The Queen and Prince Philip board their aircraft in Melbourne, Australia.

*Smiling and enjoying the ride on the royal tram in
Melbourne, Australia, 2011.*

Meeting koalas at Rainforest Walk in Brisbane, Australia, 2011.

The Queen visits the Australian War Memorial in Canberra, Australia, with Major General Steve Gower and sees a photograph of her first visit there in 1954.

The previous CHOGM had been in Port of Spain, Trinidad. The most pleasing moment of the meeting for the Queen may have been the result of a referendum held not far away in St Vincent and the Grenadines. Its prime minister, Ralph Gonsalves, wanted to make the country a republic, but its people voted decisively to keep the Queen as head of state.

The prime minister of Bermuda, Ewart Brown, had similar ambitions, but when the Queen and Prince Philip visited it on the way to Trinidad, a great crowd of 20,000 lined the road four-deep as her car passed through the capital, Hamilton.

The tour marked the 400th anniversary of Bermuda's settlement in 1609 by the English survivors of a shipwreck, and in some respects little appeared to have changed since the Queen's first visit in 1953. There were babies in silver foil crowns, the Governor wore a plumed hat, and one woman waved a Union Jack made to celebrate the Silver Jubilee of the Queen's grandfather, George V.

Other onlookers, however, accepted that things would eventually have to change. "Independence?" said one to *The Times*, "it's a natural progression. But today is exciting." By contrast, Trinidad and Tobago had become a republic in 1976, but its ties with Britain remained strong.

In her speech at the state banquet, the Queen, wearing a dress embroidered with emblems of the islands including the poinsettia and a scarlet ibis, made reference to the country's sporting prowess. She added that she was looking forward to seeing its athletes in London for the Olympics in 2012.

Then, as the CHOGM began the next day, she seamlessly switched roles from head of state to what Prince Philip called being "the Commonwealth's psychotherapist." There were 49 other world leaders present, but over the next few days few could match the stamina of this remarkably hardy octogenarian.

In Bermuda, they may be sartorial, but don't count on seeing the royal shorts at Balmoral

To their admirers, they are a cool and stylish way for the sartorially conscious male to deal with the heat of the tropics, to their detractors, nothing short of a fashion disaster. Bermuda shorts are loved or loathed, and yesterday, to his muted delight, the Duke of Edinburgh was presented with a pair.

Bright green they were, with a pair of knee-high blue woollen socks and a green patterned tie to complete the look of the Bermudian man about town. Although, from the look of slight suspicion on Prince Philip's face, it may be a little while before he starts wearing them for casual weekends at Balmoral.

"It is something you could use very easily," said a beaming David Hamshere, as he presented the Duke with the shorts. A gaggle of camera crews and photographers looked on expectantly. But the Duke has not been consort to the monarch for more than half a century without learning a thing or two.

"I'm not going to put them on now," he said, firmly. You could almost hear the sound of hopes being dashed. Still, at least Mr Hamshere knew he had the right size, as that had been sorted out when negotiations over the gift began two months ago.

Presenting a gift, and knowing that it is going to be worn are, of course, two entirely different things. Mr Hamshere, the co-owner of The English Sports Shop, a Bermudian menswear store claiming to sell 16,000 pairs of shorts every year, turned out to be a man with a very determined sales pitch. "You would definitely look very elegant in them," he told the Duke. The Duke looked unconvinced.

Made in Chile – no Bermuda shorts are actually made in Bermuda

– of Irish linen mixed with Trevira, a synthetic fabric, Mr Hamshere's shorts come in every colour one could imagine: yellow, pink, green, red, blue, even grey, and should, according to Mr Hamshere, be worn with long woollen socks, a shirt, tie and blazer. For Bermudian men, this is entirely acceptable business wear and even suitable for church. Some Bermudians get married in them.

"Bermudian men are peacocks," Mr Hamshere told *The Times*. "They are quite comfortable in their own skin, and wearing these bright colours.

"From my previous experience, I think the Duke would slip into these very comfortably. He may not wear them on Bond Street or Jermyn Street, but he would certainly wear them in Scotland."

Away from the island, the rest of the world wears its Bermudas casually. In America they first became popular in the 1950s. By the next decade, Bermudas were so accepted that President Kennedy regularly flashed the presidential knees in a pair – although he once advised Pierre Salinger, a journalist, not to wear his Bermudas because "you haven't got the legs for shorts".

But the Duke should be warned. Although they are not in any way suggestive, some cultures do not accept them. For example, *The Royal Gazette*, Bermuda's only daily newspaper, insists they remain illegal in Iraq.

However, life in Bermuda is not all shorts, sailing and rum. The second day of the state visit began with the Queen being driven in an open landau to the Anglican cathedral for a service marking the 400th anniversary of settlement. The Bishop of Bermuda, the Right Rev Patrick White, spoke forcefully about Bermuda's problems, from past slavery to the violence of today.

"Slavery," he said, "was a dark period in the island's history, which still casts its shadow over Bermuda today. Where was the Church in the middle of it all? Still baptising, burying and so on, but not rising above and challenging the practices of slavery in any significant way."

Turning to the problems of the present day, he said: "Again we find ourselves right in the middle of life in Bermuda, gradually forging an understanding of how we might work together and stem the rising tide of violence among our youth."

At the former Royal Naval Dockyard, the Queen was greeted by possibly the oldest musician ever to have performed for her, Hilda Smith, aged 102, who played *God Save the Queen* on the piano as the monarch toured the Dockyards Clocktower Building.

The Times, November 26, 2009

Prince Philip is presented with a pair of Bermuda shorts during a visit to the Naval Dockyard in Hamilton, Bermuda.

Helping to plant a palm tree in the grounds of Government House in Hamilton, Bermuda, 2009.

The Queen arrives for a state dinner hosted by Bermuda's Premier Ewart Brown and his wife Wanda Henton Brown in Bermuda, 2009.

The Queen with heads of government at the 24th CHOGM in Malta, 2015.

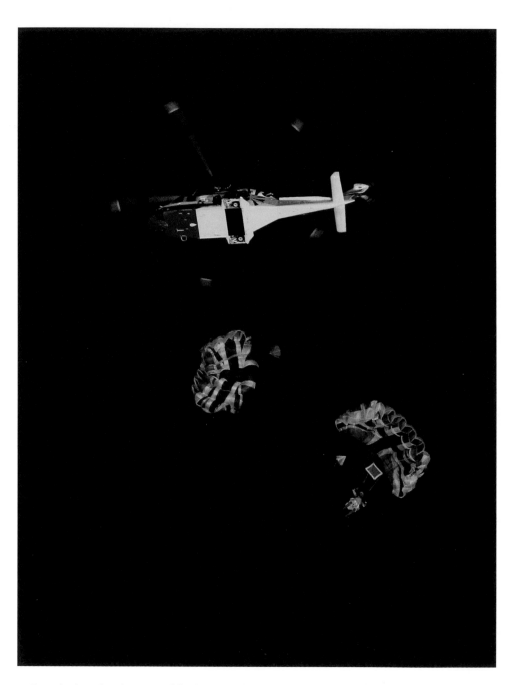

Parachutists play the parts of the Queen and James Bond during the Opening Ceremony of the London 2012 Olympic Games.

The Olympics in 2012 would confirm the standing of the Queen right around the world. There could be no stronger proof of this than the opening skit in which she pretended to parachute into the stadium besides James Bond, placing the two great icons of British identity on the same level.

The Queen's Diamond Jubilee was also celebrated the same year. It was marked in the Commonwealth by six different kinds of projects, among them one harnessing the power of sport and another encouraging leadership. The intention was increasingly evident – that preparations were being made for the Queen to leave a legacy for the future.

She had once quipped that she "needed to be seen to be believed", but after 2011 she would only make one more visit to a Commonwealth country, and that in part dictated by nostalgia.

"I feel enormously proud of what the Commonwealth has achieved, and all of it within my lifetime."

In 2015, she and Prince Philip, who was by then 94, went to Malta. The island was hosting the CHOGM, but this gave the Queen a reason to return once more to the place where she and the Duke had lived for two years as newlyweds.

The relatively carefree life that she had enjoyed from 1949 had come to an end with her accession to the throne. Nonetheless, in her speech opening the CHOGM she underscored how much she had "cherished the responsibility" of being head of the Commonwealth. "I feel enormously proud of what the Commonwealth has achieved," she said, "and all of it within my lifetime."

Queen walks Malta's memory lane

For the Queen, the memories came back one by one – a tune here, a familiar face there and, most poignant of all, a picture that in an instant brought back a time that was long past but never forgotten.

Yesterday the Queen arrived in Malta, for a visit that in theory was all about the Commonwealth. She was accompanied not just by the Duke of Edinburgh but by the Prince of Wales and the Duchess of Cornwall, a rare move that shows how determined she is that Charles should inherit her position as head of the Commonwealth.

For the Queen, the visit also had a deeper, more personal meaning, as she returned to the island where she spent some of the happiest months of her life. It was where she stayed with Prince Philip after he was posted there to serve with the Mediterranean fleet between 1949 and 1951 – carefree times for a young married couple.

At the presidential residence, the St Anton Palace, a simple watercolour painting brought it all back again. A gift from Marie-Louise Coleiro Preca, the president, it showed the Villa Guardamangia, the house in Valletta where the couple stayed with Lord Mountbatten, Prince Philip's uncle.

Since then it has fallen into disrepair, a place of crumbling stonework and peeling paint. The Maltese government wants to buy it and renovate it as a tourist attraction, but a dispute with the owners means that so far nothing has been done.

The painting by Edwin Galea, a local artist, showed the house in happier times. "Oh look," said the Queen, clearly delighted. "Guardamangia! That's very nice to have."

The Queen and the duke acknowledged that the villa had

since suffered neglect. "It looks rather sad now," the Queen said. The duke added: "It's falling down. There's some dispute about it." On a day of squally showers, the Queen was deprived of her first opportunity to meet the people of Malta again when the welcoming ceremony was moved from St George's Square to St Anton Palace. There, a military band played *Thanks For The Memory*.

At an evening reception, the people of Malta showed that they had not forgotten the Queen – and she had not forgotten them.

Elizabeth Pulé, 72, is a former nurse whose mother, Jessie Grech, had been housekeeper at the Villa Guardamangia. "She always stayed in touch with them afterwards and got invited to the Coronation," said Mrs Pulé, who is named after the Queen.

Many years later, when the Queen arrived in Malta on the Royal Yacht Britannia, Mrs Pulé held up a banner saying "Jessie was my mother" as the Queen drove through Valletta, prompting the Queen to peer out of the car in surprise. "The next day I got a call and was invited on to the yacht with my husband for an hour. She never forgot us," she said.

Last night they spoke again, and the Queen recalled her astonishment at seeing Mrs Pulé with her placard. "She is marvellous, I am so emotional," said Mrs Pulé.

Among the other old faces was Freddie Mizzi, 81, a clarinet player with the Jimmy Dowling Band when the Queen and the duke used to go dancing at the Phoenicia hotel in Valletta in 1950s. He said: "I reminded her that we used to play their favourite song, *People Will Say We're in Love*, from *Oklahoma!*, and she remembered.

"She and the duke used to dance a lot. She was always beautiful and always so nice and kind, and she hasn't changed. She is still beautiful and when you talk to her it's like talking to a member of your family."

The Times, November 27, 2015

She had meant to travel to the previous CHOGM, which was staged in Colombo. Yet after Sri Lanka's government became mired in controversy over alleged atrocities committed during the country's civil war, she opted not to attend, in what was billed diplomatically as a concession to her age.

It was the first time in more than 40 years that she had missed the conference. Prince Charles went in her stead and, in a signpost of what was to come, also accompanied her to Malta. In Kampala, in 2007, the Commonwealth had rowed back a little from the assumption that the next sovereign of the United Kingdom would automatically be the head of the Commonwealth.

Eleven years later, however, when the Queen hosted the 2018 CHOGM at Buckingham Palace and at Windsor Castle, the organisation did not demur when she asked that the Prince of Wales be allowed to "carry on the important work started by my father in 1949." A simple statement announced that Prince Charles would be the next head of the Commonwealth.

At that point, it appeared that Prince Harry was being trained up for a larger role within it, too. He had been appointed youth ambassador to the organisation, had created a highly favourable impression during visits to Africa and the Caribbean, and was about to marry a mixed-race woman, Meghan Markle.

As it proved, the Sussexes preferred another destiny, eschewing royal duties for a different kind of life in California. Over the next few years, as both Britain and the Commonwealth endured the Covid pandemic, the Queen had to deal with other blows, above all the death in 2021 of Prince Philip.

She had often paid tribute to his own work for the Commonwealth. Now it was for other hands to build on their achievements. As was shown by the Duke and Duchess of Cambridge's fraught visit in 2022 to the Caribbean, where they were met by calls for the monarchy to make reparations for slavery, and by the news that Jamaica would become a republic, the way ahead would not always be easy.

Yet without what the Queen had done to shape, nurture and bind together the Commonwealth – sustaining a highly diverse community not always harmonious but one which showed the worth of that aspiration – the road to the future would probably not be discernible at all.

Princess Elizabeth and her husband, the Duke of Edinburgh, at the Villa Guardamangia in Malta, 1949.

THE QUIET DIPLOMAT

by Valentine Low

The Queen fulfils her international role in a way that no British sovereign has done before. From her first triumphant tour as Princess Elizabeth to the delicate diplomacy of the 2015 Chinese state visit, she has met many world leaders, and they have often been highly impressed.

She still works a unique brand of magic. When the Chinese president Xi Jinping visited Britain in 2015, the palace welcome was treated by China as the sort of affirmation they could get nowhere else in the world. It had been the same in Germany that summer when Angela Merkel abandoned a meeting on the Greek economy to spend more time with her guest. And the Queen may be one of the few people capable of making Donald (and Melania) Trump seem happy to share the limelight.

Even when she has been among the most stellar players on the international stage, the Queen has shown a quiet magnetism that has remained undiminished – to say nothing of a capacity to surprise. When she and Michelle Obama put their arms around each other at a Buckingham Palace reception, it showed the Queen to be warmer and more affectionate than some have supposed, and less bound by protocol than those who surround her. The bond forged between them paved the way for a successful state visit by President Obama two years later.

Some bonds are stronger than others. When Vladimir Putin visited in 2000, he had tea with the Queen at Windsor Castle – a relatively brief visit that did not, presumably, feature any hugs. Three years later the Russian president paid a state visit that was notable, among other things, for his being 15 minutes late for the ceremonial welcome.

One of her warmest relationships was with Nelson Mandela. The South African president is reported to have been one of the few people who got away with calling her Elizabeth; she called him Nelson. They got off to a good start long before he was elected president. Recently released from prison, Mandela had been invited to the 1991 Commonwealth summit in Harare but, because he was not a head of government, he had not been invited to the Queen's banquet. Her courtiers, unsure what to do, asked her. "Let's have him," she said. They got on, it was said, "like a house on fire".

Mandela even got the Queen to behave in unQueen-like ways. On his state visit to Britain in 1996 he asked for a concert at the Royal Albert Hall instead of a banquet. When, during the rousing finale, he got up to dance, she did likewise. "Good heavens," said one establishment figure. "The Queen is dancing!"

The Queen rides with Nelson Mandela, President of South Africa, in 1996. The two had a strong friendship and he is said to have been one of the few to be on first-name terms with the monarch.

The Queen with Vladimir Putin at Windsor Castle, 2000.

With the German chancellor Angela Merkel, 2009.

The Queen with President Barack Obama, 2011.

In an era when we are accustomed to the international celebrity status of the Duchess of Cambridge, and before her Diana, Princess of Wales, it is easy to forget that the young Elizabeth had a star quality at least as great, if not greater. Crowds came out in their thousands to see her, and statesmen found themselves falling for her charms. In a post-war world short of glamour and fun there was fanciful talk of the "Faerie Princess". Later, when youth and beauty were no longer the most important weapons in her armoury, she employed her wisdom and experience to useful effect. On more than one occasion the British government owed some of its foreign policy successes to the backstage diplomacy carried out unnoticed by the Queen.

She won her first international admirers before she became Queen. As Princess Elizabeth, she undertook a tour of Canada in 1951 that included a trip to the USA. President Truman was smitten. Afterwards the British ambassador, Sir Oliver Franks, wrote to the King to say that when Truman appeared with her in public he conveyed "the impression of a very proud uncle presenting his favourite niece to his friends". Truman himself said: "When I was a little boy, I read about a fairy princess, and there she is."

His successor, Dwight Eisenhower, became a firm friend. When the Eisenhowers were guests at Balmoral in 1959 he admired some home-made drop scones and she promised to send him the recipe. Later, she wrote to the president: "Seeing a picture of you in today's newspaper standing in front of a barbecue grilling quail reminded me that I had never sent you the recipe of the drop scones which I promised you at Balmoral. I now hasten to do so and I do hope you will find them successful." She concluded: "I think the mixture needs a great deal of beating while making and shouldn't stand around too long before cooking."

Even the Russians were won over. When Nikita Khrushchev visited Britain in 1956, the Communist party general secretary likened her to "the sort of young woman you'd be likely to meet walking along Gorky Street on a balmy summer afternoon".

When Britain was negotiating to enter what was then called the Common Market, it tried to overcome French objections by inviting General Charles de

Gaulle for a state visit in 1960 to charm him into submission. He was given a ceremonial welcome and a state dinner and was delighted that all the royal family came to a banquet at the French embassy. He appreciated the Queen's fluency in French and realised, he wrote, that "she was well informed about everything, that her judgments, on people and events, were as clear-cut as they were thoughtful, that no one was more preoccupied by the cares and problems of our storm-tossed age". Unfortunately, de Gaulle still said "Non".

During her state visit to Morocco in 1980, after erratic behaviour from King Hassan II, including his failure to appear for a luncheon until 5pm, he pointed at Robert Fellowes, her assistant private secretary at the time, and said he was responsible for the "terrible muddle". The Queen rebuked him: "I'll thank you not to speak to my staff like that."

The Queen has had to put up with some fairly unsavoury guests. She was uncomfortable entertaining Nicolae Ceausescu, the Romanian leader, during his state visit in 1978; out walking her dogs in the gardens at Buckingham Palace, she hid behind a bush rather than converse with the dictator and his wife. She was most angry with President Mobutu of Zaire, who visited in 1973; his wife smuggled a small dog through customs and ordered it steak from the palace kitchens. The deputy master of the household was told: "Get that dog out of my house!" It was duly put on a plane to Brussels.

The Queen's one great advantage over most democratically elected leaders, and certainly all British statesmen, is that she has been around much longer than any of them. Her longevity proved useful in the Commonwealth crisis of 1979, when African leaders turned against Britain for what they saw as its failure to act against White-ruled Rhodesia.

The Queen with the Polish president Lech Wałęsa, 1991.

With Zimbabwe's president Robert Mugabe, 1994.

The Queen with President Bill Clinton, along with the First Lady Hillary Clinton and daughter Chelsea, 2000.

With US Secretary of State Hillary Clinton and the French president Nicolas Sarkozy, 2009.

As the former Commonwealth secretary general Sir Sonny Ramphal said: "Julius Nyerere [of Tanzania] and Kenneth Kaunda [of Zambia] and people like that from Africa were young men when she became Queen, making their way in political life. She knew them as young prime ministers and young presidents and so over many years they were friends."

The Commonwealth heads of government meeting in Lusaka, which Margaret Thatcher initially refused to attend, seemed set to be a disaster. "Britain was looked on with the greatest possible distrust," said a minister. Not the Queen, however; when she arrived the government-owned *Zambia Daily Mail* contrasted her "extraordinary loving heart" with Thatcher's lack of sympathy.

Sir William Heseltine, the Queen's deputy private secretary at the time, said that the Queen helped the foreign secretary, Lord Carrington, to win over Thatcher to his plan to persuade the conference that the Rhodesia question was best solved by Britain, not the Commonwealth.

As head of the Commonwealth, the Queen was seen as transcending national boundaries. Kaunda recalled a conversation in Lusaka: "She said, 'My friend, you and I should be careful. We are under the scrutiny of the British Prime Minister.' I looked up and Mrs Thatcher had her eyes fixed on us." Softened up by the Queen, Kaunda swept Thatcher on to the dancefloor after the opening banquet and the meeting ended with an agreement that led to the negotiations for the peaceful establishment of an independent Zimbabwe.

The Queen was brought into play during the Falklands crisis in 1982. Britain had American support for a military response to the invasion but it was important to strengthen the bond. During a stay at Windsor Castle, Ronald Reagan found the Queen "charming, down-to-earth", and went riding with her. In a speech to parliament, he confirmed his backing for the UK over the Falklands.

In her eighties the Queen still played an important role. The success of her state visit to the Republic of Ireland in 2011, when she laid a wreath to fallen Irish nationalists, was a triumph of her brand of quiet diplomacy. In 2014 it was followed by a state visit by the Irish president, Michael D Higgins, during which she shook hands with Martin McGuinness at Windsor Castle.

The important work was, perhaps, done behind the scenes. However, for many it is those moments in Dublin and Windsor that will go down in history – and the way the Queen, as ever, played her role to perfection.

Guests listen to a speech by the Queen in honour of the President of Ireland, Michael D Higgins, at a state banquet in Windsor in 2014.

The Queen with Pope John Paul II, 1982.

With President Gerald Ford, 1976.

The Queen with Emperor Hirohito of Japan, 1975.

The Queen with President George W Bush, 2007.

With Emperor Haile Selassie of Ethiopia, 1954.

The Queen making a toast at a state dinner in San Francisco, in 1983, with US president Ronald Reagan. The two got on famously, with Reagan calling her "charming" and "down-to-earth".

AFTERWORD

The Crown and
~ the Commonwealth ~
face a perilous future

The Duke and Duchess of Cambridge were looking cheerful, wholesome and sufficiently (but not excessively) regal as they walked up the red carpet into Jamaica's presidential residence. Andrew Holness, Jamaica's prime minister, warmly welcomed the royal couple. All was set for a predictable display of Commonwealth pomp, with plenty of flag-waving, handshaking and expressions of loyalty and mutual affection. Then Holness dropped a bomb, one that's likely to reverberate through the Commonwealth for decades and may change the monarchy for ever. "We're moving on," said the prime minister. "And we intend to attain in short order . . . our destiny as an independent, developed, prosperous country."

Jamaica had already signalled its intention to abandon the monarchy and become a republic, while remaining in the Commonwealth. Barbados did so last year. Of the 54 members of the Commonwealth, 34 are already republics. But Jamaica's prime minister had chosen to quit the club of the Queen's subjects on live television, with a royal on either side of him. Nearby, protesters were demanding the royal family apologise for the iniquities of slavery, the "unresolved issues" Holness referred to in his pointed welcoming remarks.

Jamaica's intention to ditch royal rule comes at a moment of deep vulnerability for the Commonwealth, with the Queen handing over the reins to her son, mounting pressure for slavery reparations powered by the Black Lives Matter movement, and Britain's imperial history under intense scrutiny. The Duchess of Sussex's claims of racism in the royal household may have exacerbated hostility in Caribbean countries. Britain's relationship with Commonwealth members, all but two of them former territories of the Empire, is in flux as never before. There are only 15 Commonwealth realms left, sovereign independent states recognising the Queen as monarch and formal head of state, including Canada, Australia and New Zealand.

Prince William managed to cling on to his diplomatic smile as Jamaica, in effect, sacked his family. But inside his polished brogues his toes must have been curling. For behind that dramatic gesture lie uncomfortable questions: Which Commonwealth nation will be next to escape the symbolic royal embrace? If the Commonwealth as an organisation is not about fealty to the Crown, or at least affection for it, what is it for? And if the royal family can no longer count on that warmth in former British territories then what, internationally, is its future role?

Visits like that of William and Kate to Jamaica are not supposed to be about protests, public assertions of political independence, "issues" and apologies. (At a dinner later the duke

Catherine, Duchess of Cambridge and Prince William, Duke of Cambridge arrive at Philip S. W. Goldson International Airport to start their royal tour of the Caribbean in March 2022.

declared "the appalling atrocity of slavery forever stains our history"). These occasions are intended to be celebrations, politically anodyne photoshoots when the royal family demonstrates that although it may no longer rule the waves it can still wave for the cameras, while discreetly drumming up trade and international goodwill.

British policymakers often thought in terms of clubs, places for like-minded people to congregate and, just as importantly, groups from which those considered uncongenial could be excluded. In the first half of the 20th century, Britain invented the largest club in the world: the Commonwealth of Nations, the intergovernmental organisation that includes 54 sovereign member states with a combined population of 2.4 billion people, almost a third of the global population, covering one fifth of the land mass.

Like all clubs in the modern age, this one has faced problems adapting to the times: changing membership, altered rules, cashflow problems, and accusations of obsolescence. Harold Macmillan, contemplating expansion of the Commonwealth in the early 1960s, asked: "Was it to be the RAC or Boodles?"

New members have been admitted and others expelled or "blackballed" (another British invention). The criteria for admission have changed. Older members tended to patronise new ones; the intake regard the old guard as archaic and old-fashioned, and occasionally break the club rules, sometimes flagrantly.

Like one of those gentlemen's clubs on Pall Mall, the Commonwealth boasts a grand address and a venerable past but the façade is crumbling, the facilities are ancient, the resources insufficient; the point obscure. Members do not care for it as they once did and some repudiate its past. Others want a greater say in the way it is run. Some want to remain members but on different terms. Like Barbados, Jamaica may renounce the Queen as head of state but is likely to remain within the Commonwealth.

Clubs grow old with their members. PG Wodehouse wrote: "I

mean, when you've got used to a club where everything's nice and cheery, and where, if you want to attract a chappie's attention, you heave a piece of bread at him, it kind of damps you to come to a place where the youngest member is about 87 and it isn't considered good form to talk to anyone unless you and he went through the Peninsular War together."

But the biggest challenge facing the Commonwealth (to extend the metaphor) is the change in club president. The Queen has zealously and jealously presided over what she called this "family of nations" since her accession but is passing the job on to new management. The Prince of Wales is her designated successor as head of the Commonwealth, and though the post is not hereditary (in theory), it seems highly likely that Prince William will succeed his father.

A former prime minister of New Zealand once famously described the Queen as "the bit of glue that somehow manages to hold the whole thing together". The royals will now have to find a new sort of adhesive or watch the club fall apart. The royal family and the Commonwealth that

The Queen stands with Prince Charles on the balcony of Buckingham Palace during the Platinum Jubilee celebrations in June 2022.

gives it much of its meaning together face a crossroads: whether to run the organisation in a way that preserves it or, like Wodehouse's club, slip into geriatric irrelevance.

The Commonwealth was shaped in the wake of decolonisation, as former British territories embraced self-government in different forms. Members of the Commonwealth have no legal obligations to each other and are instead held together through historical ties and use of the English language. The Commonwealth charter enshrines their shared values as democracy, human rights and the rule of law. In her Christmas Day 1953 broadcast, the Queen described the Commonwealth as "an entirely new conception, built on the highest qualities of the spirit of man: friendship, loyalty, and the desire for freedom and peace". On occasion, the Commonwealth has met those lofty aims. In 1961, the Commonwealth effectively ruled that respect for racial equality must be a requirement for membership (South Africa had reapplied for membership at that point, and immediately

withdrew). The Commonwealth made important contributions to progressive issues such as opposition to White minority rule in Rhodesia (now Zimbabwe). In 1995 it suspended Nigeria after it executed nine environmentalists; in 2002 it suspended Zimbabwe; in 2006 and 2009 Fiji was suspended after a military coup and the abrogation of the constitution.

> *"It is an entirely new conception, built on the highest qualities of the spirit of man: friendship, loyalty and the desire for freedom and peace."*

But at its core, the Commonwealth was less about ethics, economics and politics than sentiment, a nostalgia for past greatness. In *The Empire's New Clothes: The Myth of the Commonwealth*, Philip Murphy, director of history and policy at the Institute of Historical Research, wrote: "The idea of the Commonwealth was a great, soothing comfort blanket for the . . . dwindling band of postwar imperial enthusiasts. They could reassure themselves that the sad business of granting independence to British colonies wasn't really the end of the line. Like the souls of the faithful departed, these countries would simply join the heavenly throng of the Commonwealth and live in eternal peace and harmony."

In one of many newspaper columns he must now profoundly regret, Boris Johnson wrote in 2002 that the Queen loved the Commonwealth "partly because it supplies her with regular cheering crowds of flag-waving piccaninnies". The monarch maintained her interest in the Commonwealth and assiduously reinforced the bonds of the former Empire long after the rest of the British establishment was looking elsewhere, to the US and Europe.

Many former colonial states, and not just those with a history of slavery, decline to see the past as a cause for celebration. In India, the comforting argument that Britain brought India the railways, democracy and English has given way to a narrative in which the colonial power is seen as predominantly exploitative.

Some Brexiteers predicted that once Britain had left the EU, new trading relationships could be seamlessly re-established with former countries of the Empire, a belief based on hope rather than the economic priorities of those nations. So far, no Commonwealth trading bloc has emerged to replace the EU.

Member states may speak English but they disagree on a whole range of issues; the family squabbles constantly. Some member states still outlaw homosexuality, a throwback to the Indian Penal Code of 1860 that restricted free speech and governed sexual morality, including sex "against the order of nature". Britain may have moved on from those laws but some of its former dominions have not.

Critics point out that while the Commonwealth espouses laudable principles under royal leadership, these are routinely disregarded by some members. In 2013 Sri Lanka hosted the heads of government meeting even though the Rajapaksa regime had egregiously violated the core Commonwealth values of democracy, the rule of law and human rights. Back in 2011, the former foreign secretary Malcolm Rifkind warned: "The Commonwealth faces a very significant problem. It's not a problem of hostility or antagonism, it's more of a problem of indifference. Its purpose is being questioned, its relevance is being questioned and part of that is because its commitment to enforce the values for which it stands is becoming ambiguous in the eyes of many member states."

Most Britons today are profoundly indifferent to the Commonwealth as an institution, taking an interest only once every four years with the advent of the Commonwealth Games. The ties that once held the agglomeration together have loosened during the Queen's long reign. The 1948 British Nationality Act once confirmed the right of colonial and Commonwealth subjects to enter, work and settle in Britain, but immigration acts and nationality legislation between the 1960s and 1980s progressively closed that door.

Barbados and now Jamaica are only the latest of the Caribbean realms to pull away from the Crown:

Guyana became a republic in 1970, Trinidad and Tobago followed in 1976 and Dominica two years later. The Queen's successors are certain to face growing republican movements in the former colonies once regarded as rock-solid remainers in the Commonwealth fold. In a 1999 referendum, Australian voters rejected a proposal to establish a republic, but republicanism is officially supported by the Labour Party, the Greens and some Liberals. In 2010 Julia Gillard, the former prime minister, spoke for many Australians when she predicted that the country would become a republic after the death of the Queen: "I believe that this nation should be a republic. I also believe that this nation has got a deep affection for Queen Elizabeth."

Polls in New Zealand suggest a majority favour retaining the monarchy but more out of indifference than active enthusiasm. A recent poll found that while 70 per cent of voters want to keep the Queen as head of state, that figure drops to just over 50 per cent if and when Charles becomes King.

A survey in Canada last month showed that 49 per cent of Canadians would prefer an elected head of state, while 21 per cent would rather keep the monarchy. Of those who support a royal head of state, a third of Canadians would rather have King William V than his father, who will be Charles III.

The Duke of Cambridge attends the inaugural Commissioning Parade for service personnel from across the Caribbean at the Jamaica Defence Force in March 2022.

While the Commonwealth evolved under Queen Elizabeth II, her role as its head changed little: to stand as a symbol of agreed values and a shared past in a liberal, multiracial and multicultural association of equals. But the nature of that history is now hotly debated. The human misery that underpinned colonial power is increasingly the subject of political conflict and has led to demands for economic compensation. The political ground is shifting rapidly beneath the royal feet: in 2012 in the Solomon Islands, Prince William was carried aloft in a sedan chair by semi-clad Black people. That is not an image his handlers would permit today.

There is no guarantee that William will take over from Charles as Commonwealth head (some have urged India to assume a greater leadership role in the group), but if he does he will face a huge challenge that charm alone may not be sufficient to meet: a disparate assembly, some of whom are seceding from royal rule, with others likely to follow; a group that seems uncertain what it believes in, and unable to enforce what it does; an upswell of republicanism kept in check while the Queen is alive that may burst out when she dies; a club whose members are quitting, breaking the rules, or setting their own.

One way the monarchy could find new relevance in the Commonwealth would be to tour former imperial dominions supporting human rights defenders, promoting tolerance, environmentalism, gender equality, freedom of expression, the rights of small states and the rule of law. Around the globe, British imperialism is increasingly associated with brutal repression; the Crown might find a role in the Commonwealth by espousing everything the British Empire was not.

This week in Jamaica, Prince William said: "I strongly agree with my father, the Prince of Wales, who said in Barbados last year that the appalling atrocity of slavery forever stains our history . . . I want to express my profound sorrow. Slavery was abhorrent. And it should never have happened."

The role of the Crown in the Commonwealth was once to celebrate British history; henceforth, it may be to apologise for it. If he takes over as titular head of this group and the ruler of however many Commonwealth realms remain, William will face a far harder task than his grandmother. The pained look on his face as Jamaica's prime minister announced his country was moving on suggests he knows it.

The Commonwealth without the Queen who has headed it since 1952 is an uncertain institution; perhaps even more unclear is what a British monarchy would be without the Commonwealth club to support it.

The Times, March 25, 2022

THE WAY AHEAD

Most of this book has been about the past, a celebration of the Queen's historic role in shaping the Commonwealth and in preserving the monarchy's links with those countries it once ruled and with those that, in theory, it still does. But what about the future?

A blunt view, but not one entirely without foundation, is that the Commonwealth's role hitherto has been largely to enable the Queen to maintain that promise of service that she made at twenty-one. When the time comes for a new Head to succeed, and the agreement is that it will be Prince Charles, the moment will also be ripe for the Commonwealth to take stock and perhaps to reinvent itself.

It has several obvious problems to overcome. Two are what the function of the Head should be, and what ought to be that of the Commonwealth. A good start would be to create a more widespread understanding, even a proper definition, of the Commonwealth, and ideally a distinction between the modern club of members, many of them republics, and that of the dozen or so remaining realms which the Head will visit regularly chiefly because he is still their sovereign.

The numbers of those are dwindling, of course, with Jamaica the latest to signal that it wishes to be fully self-determining. In recent years, the debate about Britain's colonial legacy, and about its part in the slave trade, has gained much greater impetus. One role that the Commonwealth could play is to host discussion of that.

Certainly, it needs for the wider public to believe that it can achieve results rather than just be a talking shop. In the 1970s, it did seem to embody a hopeful future for many of its newly independent members, but its concrete accomplishments have been limited and its youthful radicalism has withered.

Meetings and conferences do offer useful, if less visible, benefits, but without purpose the risk is that the organisation simply lends respectability to regimes that need it.

If the Commonwealth could make use of outside perspective to reorient itself, so too it may be able to help Britain do the same. The nation which has always given the steer to the old Empire is in a muddle at present about its own identity. In truth, it has always had an uncertain relationship with its former possessions.

Most people feel little attachment to them unless they have past links – something that may have been the case even at the height of the Empire – and those that do may give more weight to the Anglocentric ones such as Australia and Canada.

Whatever the Commonwealth is going to be, it now seems clear that it will not be the oven-ready replacement for the European Union that it was cast as in the debate around Brexit. Nor are any of the more fanciful ideas for its future which have been ventured likely to fly. What, for instance, would be the advantages for India, which is not doing too badly by itself just now, in taking on a more prominent leadership role in the Commonwealth?

The future is more uncertain than it has been for many decades. And in an uncertain world one should not underestimate, as a former British prime minister, Alec Douglas-Home once observed, the usefulness of something not abundant internationally: friendship.

In the current international political climate, there is a job for the Commonwealth to do in strengthening mutual security in its regions. There are also other issues which threaten the safety of all of its members, such as climate change.

Friendship may be an intangible benefit, its meaning may alter over time, and it can be a fragile bridge on which to place hopes. Yet the photographs in this volume, and the example given for 70 years by the Head of the Commonwealth, show that it can be fostered, adapted and sustained, even between peoples with difficult pasts in common and with diverging paths into the future. That is the way ahead.

The Queen opens the 25th CHOGM in the ballroom at Buckingham Palace, 2018.

The Queen celebrates the start of the Platinum Jubilee during a reception at Sandringham House, 2022.

The Queen's Commonwealth Day Message 2022

In this year of my Platinum Jubilee, it has given me pleasure to renew the promise I made in 1947, that my life will always be devoted in service.

Today, it is rewarding to observe a modern, vibrant and connected Commonwealth that combines a wealth of history and tradition with the great social, cultural and technological advances of our time.

That the Commonwealth stands ever taller is a credit to all who have been involved. We are nourished and sustained by our relationships and, throughout my life, I have enjoyed the privilege of hearing what the relationships built across the great reach and diversity of the Commonwealth have meant to people and communities.

Our family of nations continues to be a point of connection, cooperation and friendship. It is a place to come together to pursue common goals and the common good, providing everyone with the opportunity to serve and benefit.

In these testing times, it is my hope that you can draw strength and inspiration from what we share, as we work together towards a healthy, sustainable and prosperous future for all.

And on this special day for our family – in a year that will include the Commonwealth Heads of Government Meeting and the Commonwealth Games – I hope we can deepen our resolve to support and serve one another, and endeavour to ensure the Commonwealth remains an influential force for good in our world for many generations to come.

HER MAJESTY THE QUEEN

Published March 14, 2022

Watching the RAF flypast during the Trooping the Colour from the balcony of Buckingham Palace, part of the Platinum Jubilee celebrations in June 2022.

(Left to right) the Duke of Kent, Sir Timothy Laurence, Princess Anne, the Duchess of Cornwall, Prince Charles, the Queen, Prince Louis, the Duchess of Cambridge, Princess Charlotte, Prince George, the Duke of Cambridge, the Countess of Wessex, Viscount Severn.

INDEX

Note: page numbers in **bold** refer to captions.

IMAGE CREDITS